LIVED EXPERIENCES OF HOME FORECLOSURES CONSEQUENCES ON MENTAL AND PHYSICAL HEALTH:

A PHENOMENOLOGICAL STUDY

Dr. Owusu Kizito

PAGE PUBLISHING, INC.
New York, NY

First originally published by Page Publishing, Inc. 2015

ISBN 978-1-68139-555-5 (pbk)
ISBN 978-1-68139-556-2 (digital)

Printed in the United States of America

Abstract

The rising rate of home foreclosures that stands at approximately 1 in 92 households in the United States has raised a national alarm. Medical issues account for approximately half of all home foreclosure filings, and it appears that approximately 1.5 million American homeowners would lose their homes to foreclosure every year. The qualitative phenomenological study involved investigating the lived experiences of the consequences of home foreclosures on the physical and mental illness of northern New Jersey homeowners. The research questions asked included what were the lived experiences of physical and mental health decline following home foreclosure and how did the participant's perceive their physical and mental health decline affected their family members? Four core themes were revealed from the study. The four themes included foreclosure process resulting in hospitalization of family and foreclosure associated with the lack of family's health insurance, family health and the foreclosure process, and foreclosure and the negligence of doctor's prescription, foreclosure as perceived loss of money and finally homeownership, displacement, and housing instability as a reason for depression. The current phenomenological research study of the lived experiences of home foreclosures on 25 homeowners in the process of foreclosure has added to the body of knowledge because it highlighted the stressors, reasons, and causes. The study provides a framework for local practitioners and decision makers in identifying the consequences on the physical and mental health of the participants and their families and providing a workable foreclosure response system.

Dedication

This dissertation is dedicated to the millions of homeowners who are victims of home foreclosures. The project uncovered a unique understanding of the possible negative consequences of home foreclosures on the mental and physical health of affected homeowners. Your quiet suffering has been recognized, and I look forward to the implementation of the mitigating strategies recommended in this qualitative research. Additionally, I dedicate this project to my wife, Arita, and daughter, Roselyn, and our twin boys, Stevie and Eddie. My wife has been my rock through this program. I admire her patience, endurance, empathy, wisdom, encouragement, thoughtfulness, and dedication to the pursuit of excellence in her husband. I thank God that my wife was able to support me through the program and I am very grateful. My daughter, Roselyn, was just born when I started the program and she now identifies her father as a scholar who likes to study! She is such a joy and she looks forward to going to school every day as a three-year-old. To my father, Stephen, and mother, Rose, I especially dedicate this dissertation to you because of your constant reminder of the value and contribution of education. I could not have accomplished this without your foresight. I ask for God's blessings on both of you. To my brothers and sisters, I want to dedicate this dissertation to you to serve as inspiration and encouragement that, with God, all things are possible.

Acknowledgments

To my committee members: Dr. Vineeta Kapoor, my mentor and inspiration for providing leadership and significant support in my dissertation journey into successful completion; Dr. Brent Muirhead, for providing excellent critique that helped me transform my dissertation into a useful project; and Dr. Everett Poore, for his guidance, meaningful and unwavering support to make t his dissertation an excellent piece of scholarly work. My special thanks to Dr. Johnny Morris for his excellent leadership before his retirement as my dissertation chair. I am grateful for the support of my academic advisor Kris Moller and academic counselor Melissa Fuentes, for their constant reminder of excellence and focus on my studies. Dr. Kathy Jones provided critique, insight, and wisdom into this manuscript, of which I am thankful. Special thanks to Jackie Johnson, my financial counselor; family members; close friends; and associates for their inspiration, support, best wishes, and sacrifices in making this dissertation and doctoral journey a success. Above all, I thank God for his faithfulness!

Contents

List of Tables

CHAPTER 1

Introduction

A critical national concern has developed because of the growing number of home foreclosures in recent years, which currently stands about one in 92 households in the United States (Realty Trac, 2007). This situation has wide social implications, including unknown health-related consequences to the individuals involved. According to Robertson, Egelhof, and Hoke (2008), medical crises are among the major causes of home foreclosures, along with other factors such as rising interest rates, loose lending, a flat real estate market, and irresponsible borrowers. Approximately half of all home foreclosure filings result from family medical crises, and approximately 1.5 million American homeowners could undergo foreclosure each year.

It appears the threat of losing a home can be stressful enough to make a homeowner sick, and researchers have shown a correlation exists between foreclosure rates and people's health using the states of Arizona, New Jersey, Florida, and California as examples (Kalita, 2011). Kalita (2011) explained that researchers at Princeton University and Georgia State University found that a 7.2 percent and 8.1 percent rise in emergency visitations and hospitalizations occurs for hypertension and diabetes, respectively, among people aged 20 to 49 years, and 12 percent more anxiety-related hospital visits occur for every increase of 100 foreclosures in the same age category. Thirty-nine percent more hospital visits occur for suicide attempts for the same rise in foreclosures among the same age group.

The consequences of home foreclosures on affected families include eliminating the entire savings of the homeowners and causing unknown health-related concerns (Robertson et al., 2008). Other repercussions involve leaving significant debt on the homes they no longer own and having harmful consequences on neighborhoods and local communities. Home foreclosures reduce the return on investment for investors and lenders and upset the national goal of home-ownership that influences social policy. As explained by Robertson et al. (2008), medical crises account for about half of all home foreclosure filings, which was previously unknown to policy makers and scholars; equally unknown are the health ramifications to persons undergoing foreclosure. The study involved investigating the lived experiences of the potentially negative consequences home foreclosures have on the physical and mental health of northern New Jersey homeowners. The study focused on the physical and mental health consequences and involved sampling 25 individuals in the process of foreclosure to explore their health consequences and analyze the findings to provide recommendations. The results may be particularly useful for local legal practitioners, state and local officials, and other decision makers in suggesting solutions for a workable local foreclosure response system.

Background of Problem

Shetty and Kroleski (2010) observed that a steady increase in mortgage defaults is taking place, and without intervention from federal, state, and local agencies; the judiciary; or lending institutions, the damages to families because of foreclosure will continue to rise. A direct result of foreclosure, the decline in home values, and the loss of equity in homes is the displacement of homeowners and their families (Shetty & Kroleski, 2010). Lenders are incurring losses and are becoming hesitant to lend to prospective homebuyers, resulting in a dismal economic future for the United States and restricted financial well-being for both affected and unaffected families.

The mortgage crisis was the result of overeager lenders and borrowers motivated by greed or ignorance, as well as real estate brokers, appraisers, and mortgage brokers. During the period from 2000 to the end of 2006, a sharp rise in home prices in the United States occurred; homeownership increased remarkably because lower income families were able to buy houses using subprime loans (Kingsley, Smith, & Price, 2009). That is, the situation developed because lenders made loans to unqualified borrowers, which affected responsible borrowers because home values in their neighborhoods declined. Homeowners confronted with costly home repairs, college tuition, or other costs were not able to refinance because of the decrease in home values, and without substantial equity in their homes, they had to default on their mortgages to pay for the urgent matters.

Problem Statement

The general problem is that even though "stress is a normal part of everyday life,…the high levels of anxiety, shame, uncertainty, and fear likely associated with home foreclosure may contribute to a host of physical and mental illness" (Kingsley et al., 2009, p. 3). The health-related concerns of home foreclosures on families are mostly unexplored (Housing Program of Jefferson Parish, 2007). The specific problem is that the potential deleterious consequences of home foreclosures on physical and mental health remain generally unknown. Families in foreclosure may have more health problems than do their unaffected counterparts (Childs, 2008). Kalita (2011) found a rise of 100 foreclosures accounted for 12 percent more emergency and hospital visits for the individuals involved, and for an increase of 100 foreclosures, 39 percent more suicide-attempt patients went to emergency rooms and were hospitalized.

Purpose Statement

The purpose of this qualitative phenomenological study was to examine the participant's lived experiences of the possible negative consequences of home foreclosures on physical and mental health in northern New Jersey. To fulfill the objectives of the study, 25 homeowners in the process of foreclosure participated in interviews to investigate the as-yet undetected health-related concerns brought about by home foreclosures. Older adults might especially feel the consequences of foreclosure because of the chronic health conditions that make relocation and adjustment to new neighborhoods stressful. The most intense demonstration of the possible impairment to mental health is the suicide rate of individuals before, during, or after foreclosure with its related financial problems (Kingsley et al., 2009).

Significance to the Field of Study and Leadership

The end users of the study might include city and metropolitan leaders, as well as practitioners, creating appropriate foreclosure responses and introducing changes in policy at the local, state, and national levels. According to Kingsley et al. (2009), a sound and workable local foreclosure response system must entail (a) developing an organized foreclosure response approach, (b) preventing foreclosures and keeping families in their houses, (c) stabilizing communities, and (d) helping families bounce back.

In the development of a coordinated foreclosure response strategy, task forces in communities can help to pull together and enhance local actions to manage foreclosure issues by organizing for the foreclosure response, strengthening the policies of state and local governments, developing a local action plan, and assessing the progress of the actions implemented (Kingsley et al., 2009). Establishing such organizations requires the identification of the groups already involved in resolving some features of the foreclosure crisis, which could include real estate agents, developers, legal-aid firms, banks, political officials, advocates, philanthropic groups, housing counseling, and nonprofit community development agencies. In some areas, people are willing to work together; whereas, individuals in other communities might need more publicity and education to inform stakeholders of the need to join an effectively coordinated response strategy. Kingsley et al. (2009) noted, "Since many of the laws and regulations that will determine the effectiveness of foreclosure response occurs at the state level, it is important that priority be given to organizing at that level" (p. 23).

To address the foreclosure crisis, the United States federal government and individual states must develop a comprehensive foreclosure response strategy and broad-reaching task forces must exist in states. The foreclosure task forces should have diverse membership that might include attorneys, developers, business leaders, nonprofits, real estate agents, business leaders, and government officials. These associations also might exist at the regional and local levels (Mallach, 2008).

In an attempt to strengthen the state and local policy environment, Mallach (2008) suggested officials can implement the following to effect changes: for a fair foreclosure process, the laws should (a) prevent foreclosure rescue schemes that may be deceptive, (b) support entities that convey foreclosed properties to responsible owners, (c) encourage mortgage companies to pursue foreclosure alternatives, and (d) provide funding and support to local counseling agencies in their activities. Developing a local action strategy will include foreclosure prevention, neighborhood spillover effects, and approaching as well as assisting the recovery of affected families. Reliable data are necessary to address these foreclosure problems across neighborhoods. Entities dealing with the foreclosure crisis should prepare regular reports to assess the success of their efforts. According to Kingsley et al. (2009), some cities have computer-accessible records on foreclosure notifications as well as transfers of monthly title reports on some features of the foreclosure crisis. These might be useful for cities, counties, or particular communities regarding the number of real-estate–owned properties in the process of foreclosure.

Counseling homeowners to remain current on their mortgage payments can help prevent foreclosures and keep families in their homes. Foreclosure counselors might suggest loan modifications with mortgage companies when homeowners are unable to keep up with their regular payments and help them set up an affordable payment plan. As a last resort, the homeowners can become renters in their foreclosed homes under an arrangement with the bank. Kingsley et al. (2009) noted a workable foreclosure prevention system should include (a) a program that reaches out to homeowners in imminent risk of default and advises them to seek responsible housing counseling; (b) the continuing development of nonprofit housing counseling agencies with a proven record of success and working relationships with lenders, servicers, and government agencies; (c) access to the available avenues that enable nonprofit housing agencies to help at-risk homeowners overcome temporary emergencies, including solution options with servicers; and (d) the availability of legal assistance to ensure the successful resolution of their delinquent mortgages.

The main goals of neighborhood stabilization programs are to stop the damaging effects of foreclosures on communities and facilitate healthy housing market conditions. The local government officials can accomplish the goals by securing and maintaining vacant properties. The local governments can help to preserve such properties by initially pressuring the banks to take care of them; still, the state may maintain these abandoned areas if the banks fail to do so (Kingsley et al., 2009).

Those involved in helping foreclosed families recover must give consideration to homeowners who may still be financially capable of maintaining an alternate residence as well as to displaced renters. Emergency housing assistance, financial or other types, might be necessary to help the most troubled and vulnerable homeowners (e.g., those undergoing illness, family stress, or job loss) and renters. They might need both housing assistance and in-kind assistance such as food and clothing. According to Kingsley et al. (2009), a wider range of social services may be necessary to help homeowners in the long term, and these may include:

1. Counseling on family financial management and, for some, help preparing for and finding new jobs.
2. Legal assistance with housing and other issues.
3. Special programs in the schools to help the children of displaced families cope with the transitions and,
4. Services to deal with severe issues like mental health problems, spousal abuse, and drug addiction that may have been exacerbated by the displacement (p. 38).

Affected homeowners might benefit from advice on how to restore their credit by helping them learn better financial management skills, how to create a budget, and how to stick with realistic plans in repairing their credit histories (Kingsley et al., 2009). Because of the urgency of the foreclosure situation and its recent nature, adequate information is not yet available to ascertain its impact on families, even though sufficient literature exists on the incidence, causes, and implications of the foreclosure crisis for the financial system (Kingsley et al., 2009).

A sense of urgency is therefore appropriate for researchers to gather information and to assess and discuss evidence for stakeholders. One hurdle is that even with considerable data about the impact of foreclosures on families, those affected are difficult to identify and track after they receive a first notice from the bank or mortgage company initiating foreclosure proceedings.

A primary obstacle is gaining access to the list of individuals facing foreclosure to interview them. The problem arises because individuals can only obtain a listing of addresses at the time of the foreclosure sale from commercial and local sources or public records. Assembling a list of addresses for the affected families for a useful survey also tends to be expensive. Kingsley et al. (2009) explained two ways to undertake the issue. First, a researcher might review and use the previous literature of families required to move because of troubles in their lives such as illness, family changes, circumstances leading to eviction, and loss of a job. Second, the researcher might interview employees of legal service groups or foreclosure counseling agencies serving families at the brink of foreclosure.

According to CoreLogic (2013), New Jersey is second of the five highest states with foreclosure inventory as a percentage of mortgaged homes, at 6.0 percent. New Jersey was a suitable case for the study because of its high inventory; it is just behind Florida, which as the highest inventory of foreclosures at 8.8 percent and well above the national average rate in 36 states of 2.6 percent. Researchers at the U.S. Department of Housing and Urban Development (HUD, 2013) classified New Jersey among seven states with very high rates of correlation between Equifax 90-day delinquencies (correlation of 0.80 or higher) and HUD's foreclosure rate estimates. Analysts at RealtyTrac (2013) estimated that 1 in every 1,444 homes in the state of New Jersey is in foreclosure. Essex County and Union County, where the mortgage foreclosure study took place, have estimates of one in every 1,314 and 1 in every 1,233 homes in foreclosure, respectively.

Nature of Study

According to Garson (2002), "Qualitative research designs strive for in-depth understanding of subjects through such techniques as participant observation or narrative analysis, or they may strive for in-depth understanding of texts through such methods as exegesis or deconstruction" (p. 294). The present study involved investigating the possible pernicious consequences of home foreclosures on the mental and physical health of northern New Jersey families. In an attempt to achieve this goal, the study involved interviewing 25 homeowners in the process of foreclosure. The phenomenological approach made it possible for the participants to tell their own story.

The researcher adapted the phenomenological technique to achieve knowledge based on the lived experiences of individuals during the period after health issues became apparent because of their home foreclosures. According to Giorgi (1997), phenomenology refers to the phenomenon of consciousness and the total number of lived experiences that pertain to a single individual. The current study included Giorgio's descriptive phenomenological method with a clear structure.

According to Kingsley et al. (2009), Coulton noted in conducting a qualitative phenomenological study on a research problem such as this, a researcher might find a list of potential subjects by:

1. Acquiring a list of properties that just recently entered the foreclosure process in a city (i.e., notice of foreclosure had been sent but sheriff's sale had not yet occurred);
2. Selecting a sample from that list and recruiting families in a short time; and
3. Conducting…interviews with all the families (p. 40).

Coulton further indicated the surveys should "cover changes in living arrangements, neighborhood quality, family economic status, employment, material hardships, physical and mental health, and children's schooling and activities" (p. 40). Coulton noted it is imperative to collect historical data on how a family came to be in a foreclosed situation. The survey should also account for rental history and leasing arrangements for renters. Researchers must conduct the study in several cities because of different market environments.

The interview-and-observation approach was the best choice for the qualitative study. The format for the interviews included telephone, online interview (chat room), and sitting face-to-face. Interviewing had the advantage of flexibility through the ability to reach a greater data depth by following up on clues for answers with semistructured questions (Strauss & Myburgh, 2001). The acts of asking, witnessing, interpreting, and knowing are the four phases of qualitative research (Stein & Makowski, 2004). To examine and obtain awareness of the subjects' lived experiences, the study involved all four phases. Kuipers (1994) posited qualitative simulation involves locating all the behaviors consistent with the knowledge in the model, and researchers who use qualitative models are more capable of expressing the states of incomplete knowledge about continuous mechanisms than are those who use traditional models. The qualitative research inquiry used in this analysis helped to explain the lived experiences of the respondents. In contrast, the quantitative research design was not applicable in this case because the research involved participants in a real-world situation. People frequently operate differently if the researcher artificially manipulate, control, or subject them to systematic observation and appraisal, as in a genuine experimental design.

Deciding the cause and the effect might be difficult when a relationship exists between two variables. The fact that two or more factors relate does not always signify a cause-and-effect relationship. They could easily relate to another factor not recognized or perceived. Controlled selection of subjects is not allowable in comparative studies in natural situations. Quasi-experimental quantitative research is practically impossible because finding groups of individuals who are similar in every way except for their contact with one variable is exceedingly problematic.

Research Question

The specific problem was that the potential adverse consequences of home foreclosures on physical and mental health are unknown. The two main research questions investigated were as follows:

Research Questions:

1. What were the lived experiences of physical and mental health decline following home foreclosure?
2. How did the participant's perceive their physical and mental health decline affected their family members?

Theoretical Lens

This section contains the major ideas that supported the research study. It also includes certain basic assumptions and an explanation of how the phenomenological study came together. Kingsley et al. (2009) described three major categories of foreclosure-related impacts on affected families, including (a) displacement and housing instability; (b) financial vulnerability and economic difficulty; and (c) personal and family tension, broken relationships, and poor health. According to humanist psychologist Maslow, people act in order to achieve certain needs, including physiological needs, security needs, social needs, esteem needs, and self-actualizing needs (Maslow, 1943). Maslow's hierarchy of needs is a relevant assumption because people have an inborn desire to be self-actualized and to be all they can be. To achieve the ultimate self-actualizing goals, individuals must first meet a number of more basic needs, such as food, safety, love, and self-esteem. Home foreclosures threaten even these more basic goals.

According to Pelletiere and Wardrip (2008), it is necessary to know a family's tenure type (i.e., whether the family rents or owns a home) to see the potential impact of foreclosure on them. Because rental units carried a significant share of foreclosed properties as the foreclosure crisis unfolded, policy concerns began to shift away from renters and focused almost entirely on owners. Nationally, rental share accounts for approximately 38 percent, but it can be as high as 60 percent in some places such as New York City (Center for Responsible Lending, 2007).

According to Moreno (1995), the foreclosure process may be the first step on the road to precarious housing for former renters or homeowners. Fellowes (2006) indicated, "The financial losses associated with foreclosure are substantial. For the homeowners, credit ratings are damaged, which affects their ability to move on to a new home and lessens their ability to get loans for other purchases" (p. 13). The effect on renters is equal. Researchers for Tenants Together (2009) indicated the consequences of foreclosure on tenants: (a) evicted through no fault of their own; (b) denied information about what is going on with their homes; (c) evicted without receiving 60-day notice; (d) forced to live without water, gas, or electricity; (e) cannot reach owners to get repairs done; (f) losing their security deposits; (g) subject to rent skimming;

(h) victims of fraud and deceptive practices; (i) credit damaged; (j) unable to get legal services; and (k) forced into homelessness.

Displacement and housing instability. According to Hartley (2010), Campbell, Giglio, and Pathak analyzed the sale price of a home in Massachusetts and determined that a foreclosure sale lowers prices about 27 percent to comparable properties as well as lowers the selling prices of other nonforeclosure houses at a distance of 260 feet by 1 percent for each foreclosed property. Thus, 10 foreclosed properties in a neighborhood could reduce the sale price of a nonforeclosure property by 10 percent. This makes the effect significant. Eggum, Porter, and Twomey (2008) observed that foreclosures continue to outpace loan modifications in spite of their identification as a preferred strategy for effective foreclosure mitigation.

Financial insecurity and economic hardship. Financial stress may be a major contributor to domestic violence, and occasions of spousal or child abuse can increase in homes undergoing the foreclosure process (Kingsley et al., 2009). Caner and Wolff (2004) asserted that, including individual retirement accounts, approximately 46 percent of households in the United States had no more than $5,000 in liquid assets, demonstrating that some homeowners were on the financial edge. In a survey of 60,000 homeowners conducted by the Homeownership Preservation Foundation, the following events push families over the edge of foreclosure:

Thirty-two percent experience job loss; 25 percent experience health crisis; 85 percent have already missed one mortgage payment; 50 percent have already missed two payments; most have no savings and no available credit, and their extended families have limited resources; most have first-time loans; and most loans are less than three years old; they may have already been refinanced two or three times. (Ackerman, 2010, p. 13)

The crucial assumption was that chapter 13 homeowners in financial trouble have incomes that are sufficient and will allow them to make future mortgage payments and manage other living expenses, which are requirements to receive bankruptcy discharge and take care of defaults on their mortgage requirements. This is evident in the anti-modification rule under the bankruptcy code, which stipulates that people in debt through bankruptcy cannot change or adjust the terms of their home mortgages, even though the general rules that involve modifying claims in bankruptcy permit debtors to modify the rights of secured and unsecured creditors that might include changing the schedule of payments or reducing the contract interest rate according to U.S. bankruptcy code 11 U.S.C. §1322(b)(2). This situation restricts modifications and makes it practically impossible for debtors with mortgage payments that are unaffordable to keep their houses from foreclosure by filing for bankruptcy.

The requirements of chapter 13 bankruptcy for financially handicapped homeowners do not permit them to be any better. As Eggum et al. (2008) explained, these people must live on a stringent budget for up to 5 years, and if their income does not increase during that time, the family may have at best a fixed housing expense or increasing mortgage payments that limit their ability to manage unexpected expenses. The chapter 13 repayment plan might continue the financial hardship of homeowners over the period, prolong the family's financial distress, and eventually cause them to lose the home to foreclosure.

Personal and family stress, disrupted relationships, and ill health. Feelings of powerlessness and victimization arise in adults experiencing foreclosures (Lashley, Maudry, Jeffers, & Davis, 2009); the affected parents and guardians undergoing foreclosure might blame themselves; their guilt might lead to cognitive imbalance with the possibility of depressive symptoms. A direct impact of foreclosures or homelessness on school-aged children is a decline in their academic performance. The children will experience the effects of the relocation or homelessness on their scholastic achievement because of the displacement as well as financial stresses (Moen, 1979); the children will unfailingly encounter traumatic and distressing conditions by changing schools in such circumstances and losing their friends. Similarly, they might be upset by having to share a room or space with other family members after having their own rooms or even by moving with their family to a shelter. Butler (2008), the researchers of *Educating the Homeless* (2008), and Lashley et al. (2009) noted schoolchildren who frequently change locations predictably have poor performance in school and can lose progress in their academic achievements. Butler noted the children might develop behavioral problems as well. According to the reporters of *Educating the Homeless* (2008), every move by a homeless or frequently moving child makes him or her vulnerable to 6 months of falling behind academically, with more than a quarter of highly mobile children repeating a grade.

Affected families might need to move from well-maintained communities to poorer neighborhoods, leading to fear, disbelief, feelings of anxiety, hopelessness, and distress. Riley and Eckenrode (1986) noted the stress experienced by affected families in foreclosure and undergoing fiscal constraints might affect members of their extended family and friends. Individuals with lower levels of personal resources, both material and psychological, experience greater stress when their spouse or significant other undergoes unfortunate life events, and they might find limited support from their social ties (Riley & Eckenrode, 1986). The trauma of losing a house can cause fear, confusion, and shame and be damaging to the physical, mental, and emotional health of the afflicted family (Kingsley et al., 2009).

Moen (1979) noted the effects of prolonged unemployment could promote a potential role conflict in the household if the wife takes over the role as the breadwinner vacated by her spouse. Such conditions might precipitate marital problems in the form of desertion, separation, or divorce, or they might encourage adolescent children to leave the home to take care of themselves prematurely. The overall effect is the sudden change in the economic status of the family. Ross and Huber (1985) recognized that the emotional well-being of husbands in their traditional role of breadwinner and wives in their role of family caretaker has ties to their ability to meet these family obligations; individuals unable to function in these roles might undergo significant stress.

Definition of Terms

Bankruptcy: Bankruptcy is a legal proceeding that involves a person or business unable to repay outstanding debts. The federal law allows a trustee to manage the individual's assets to pay off the outstanding debts (HUD, 2013). Bankruptcy filing by an individual often results in the internal transfer of business to the service provider's bankruptcy department or to an organization managing defaults.

Forbearance: Forbearance is a special plan created by a mortgage company to temporarily suspend payments or modify payments on a certain schedule, typically lasting for three to twelve months, to cure mortgage default.

Foreclosure: According to HUD (2013), foreclosure is the operation through which a bank or mortgage company transfers the title of real property in which it had interest through involuntary or forced sale of the property as a means of defraying the debt.

Loan modification: Modification of a loan happens "when a lender agrees to modify the terms of a mortgage without refinancing the loan" (HUD, 2013, "Modification" section, para.1). Modifications may include changing interest rates, which usually entails lower interest rates from the original rates or from the term of the loan.

Real estate owned: Real estate owned is in effect after a bank, mortgage company, or other party owns the property after a successful foreclosure sale (HUD, 2013).

Assumptions

The current study included human participants who willingly shared their beliefs and attitudes to provide meaning to the researcher's inquiries. A crucial assumption of the analysis tied directly to the behaviors of the respondents; that is, the researcher assumed the interviewees would respond to the questions in a straightforward, candid, and truthful manner. Because participation was on a voluntary basis, this assurance was suitable. Leedy and Ormrod (2010) noted research participants possess the experience and memory to answer such questions. The final assumption was the 25 selected respondents would represent the complete population, and the researcher met the assumption by conducting individual interviews.

Scope

Generally, the study involved investigating the unknown health-related consequences of home foreclosures in the state of New Jersey. Specifically, the researcher sampled and interviewed homeowners going through foreclosure in several counties in all parts of New Jersey. Even though any number of affected homeowners might have been in these areas, the researcher interviewed only those willing and able to provide the information necessary during foreclosure.

Limitations

A limitation of this project was the possibility that the interviewees did not provide honest answers to the questions asked. Some people might have intentionally provided incorrect answers that might have adversely affected the analysis and results of the study. An additional limitation was the researcher's experience as a housing counselor and the possible introduction of bias into the study because he regularly works with distressed homeowners undergoing foreclosure. The researcher accounted for the bias by applying the hermeneutic of revisiting the data obtained from the participants (bracketing) to evolve his understanding of the themes from the study (Fischer, 2009). The researcher adopted a stance of neutrality in undertaking the phenomenon studied to ensure valid, reliable, meaningful, and confirmable findings. The researcher also balanced his bias as a housing counselor by exercising judgment on the importance of the study and the need to remain objective (Rajendran, 2001).

Delimitation

Delimitations existed in the current study. The focus of the study was studying the lived experience of 25 homeowners in the process of foreclosure and the health issues and negative impacts of foreclosure. The participants may be of a certain category or population, which makes study not generalizable. For example, the study did not include struggling homeowners using their properties for both residential and commercial purposes. The analysis did not include the owners of foreclosed commercial property. The study is not generalizable to other populations because of the small sample size and geographic location.

General Conclusion

The effect of home foreclosure on families can be devastating (Kingsley et al., 2009). The study addressed the outcomes of foreclosure on such families and involved using the lessons learned to address similar future foreclosure crises effectively. Chapter 2 will discuss the literature concerning those events or issues such as illness, divorce, or job loss that can cause personal and family stress as well as poor outcomes for families facing home foreclosure.

Review of the Literature

The purpose of this qualitative phenomenological study was to examine the participants' lived experiences of the potential negative consequences of home foreclosures on physical and mental health among people living in northern New Jersey using transcribed semistructured and taped interviews. The focus of this chapter is on the literature concerning those events or issues such as illness, divorce, or job loss that can cause personal and family stress as well as poor outcomes for families facing foreclosure. Fischer and Kittleson (2000) defined stress as resulting from a person's perception that an event in life, a situation, or a particular circumstance is overwhelming and is greater than his or her ability to cope. Fischer and Kittleson (2000) noted further that situations, events, negative family dynamics, and interactions that occurred during childhood make an individual singularly susceptible to stress.

Armatrading (1999); Gwynne (1992); and Larsen, Wilson, and Beley (1994) asserted the precipitating factors that cause health issues and adverse family relationships include job insecurity, foreclosure, or savings and loans collapse, with their devastating effects including the dislocation of families. Job insecurity and work intensification appear to affect the general health and family relationships of the individuals involved (Armatrading, 1999). Armatrading further indicated employees who enjoy supportive relationships from their managers tend to experience less work-related stress, but the job insecurity remains. Gwynne noted economic hardship causes people to experience emotional problems such as fear when financial insecurities exist.

Larsen et al. (1994) noted the slow recovery from the recession is a major stressor for a number of American families. An untold number of Americans will feel their security slipping away as many government agencies and businesses restructure and downsize their operations in response to the current economic realities. These insecurities may result from the threat of job loss; increase in job responsibilities due to layoffs of their coworkers, which results in changes to their job descriptions; and reduced potential for promotion, cutbacks or salary freezes, and forced relocation.

Historical Overview
of Poor Outcome from Foreclosures

Poor outcomes will occur for families who suffer foreclosure on their properties. "Households [enter] foreclosure primarily when a precipitating event such as divorce, job loss, illness, or accident dramatically [changes] the family's financial situation" (Kingsley et al., 2009, p. 6). Further, heightened personal and family stress intensifies marital troubles, health problems, and negative actions such as child abuse, substance abuse, and other addictions (Kingsley et al., 2009). These effects may be difficult to document, but they have long-term consequences.

According to Wagner, Wolfe, Rotnitsky, Proctor, and Erickson (2000), stress causes damage to bodily systems, including the mental well-being of those caught in the midst of the crisis. Some distressed homeowners developing mental health issues from the foreclosure process might even attempt suicide. Childs (2008) mentioned the feelings of depression that occur when people lose their home to foreclosure because home ownership represents stability for an individual or family and its loss causes feelings of failure. Lashley et al. (2009) and Nebehay (2008) noted World Health Organization researchers warned appropriately that the financial and economic crisis would likely escalate and result in increased mental health issues, including suicide, among individuals struggling to come to terms with poverty and unemployment. Older Americans may particularly be vulnerable to the stressful effects of foreclosures because of chronic health problems (Smith & Ferryman, 2006). Indeed, relocation and adjusting to new neighborhoods are particularly difficult for the elderly and individuals with qualified health. Along these lines, Ross and Huber (1985) surveyed a certain population and discovered that retired seniors might experience fatigue, insomnia, and feelings of hopelessness because of high taxes and changes in the economic order.

According to Kingsley et al. (2009), financial stress might be a major contributor to domestic violence, and cases of spousal or child abuse could increase in homes experiencing the burden of foreclosure. Caner and Wolff (2004) explained approximately 46 percent of American families have as little as $5,000 in liquid assets, including IRAs, which indicated some families are at the brink of financial disaster. In a survey of 60,000 homeowners, researchers for the Homeownership Preservation Foundation (Ackerman, 2010) found the following circumstances might put individuals at risk of foreclosure: 25 percent resulted from a health crisis; 32 percent resulted from a job loss; 50 percent had already missed two mortgage payments and 85 percent had already missed one; most had first-time home loans; almost all had no savings, no accessible credit, and few assets available in their extended families; most had already refinanced two or three times; and virtually all loans were less than three years old. Having valid health insurance is an important consideration in the medical issues surrounding foreclosure. In fact, Duchon et al. (2001) discovered that up to one fourth of families not having health insurance might experience significant changes in their lifestyle to pay medical bills, even with just one member lacking health insurance. Watson, Jorge, Cohen, and Seifert (2007) revealed 53 percent of St. Louis, Missouri, respondents reported their medical debt resulted in housing problems.

According to Lashley et al. (2009), foreclosures affect both adults and children in households that experience foreclosure. Regardless of their psychological health before the crisis, high degrees of stress affect both grownups and children and last for extended periods. Such a situation can develop into enduring psychiatric ailments (Lashley et al., 2009). These authors noted children in afflicted households face the effects of foreclosures and associated financial problems, indicating that mental health practitioners need to develop workable strategies to empower family members to develop resiliency in managing their current economic reality. The children might exhibit psychiatric symptoms, or the impact might be evident in their emotional growth. Maikranz, Steele, and Forehand (2003) found that some children might develop social functioning difficulties or demonstrate subclinical levels of depression. Maikranz et al. (2003) also discovered urban Black youths are particularly susceptible to symptoms of depression and later psychosocial functioning because they experience frequent exposure to high-risk environments, including violence, drug use, and poor housing conditions in their communities. Such extremes may place the children at a greater risk of behavioral and emotional problems.

The foreclosure crises have resulted in an increase of severe mental and neurological disorders, making it necessary for society to pay a greater degree of attention to addressing the psychological and social effects of the damaged parties.

As discovered in one study ("Mental Health: Keeping Your Emotional Health," 2002), stress and family problems might trigger mental illness; when a family experiences a tragedy, its members often develop some form of mental or emotional impairment. Lashley et al. (2009) posited economic loss or job stress might result in heart diseases, depression, and anxiety and these may be serious enough to warrant hospitalization. The foreclosure catastrophe in the United States has contributed to an increase in incapacitating mental and neurological disorders.

Lashley et al. (2009) described several possible outcomes of stress associated with foreclosure. The first possible outcome is the feeling of powerlessness and victimization in the adults experiencing foreclosures. The debilitating effects include affecting the subsystems of both parents and adults and making them feel hopeless, even persecuted. Gray, Maguen, and Litz (2004) compared this to the grief experienced by individuals and families who lost relatives and close friends in the September 11, 2001, terrorist strike on the buildings of the World Trade Center. Their struggle to adjust to their bereavement after the event caused irritability, anger, and bitterness and influenced their relationship with family and peers. Parents and parent figures undergoing foreclosure might blame themselves, and these feelings of guilt might result in cognitive imbalance with the possibility of depressive symptoms. Gray et al. observed that when some people experience adversities in their lives, they find it difficult to adjust to their new reality, which might result in sustained difficulties.

The second possible outcome of stress associated with foreclosure is that homelessness will affect the academic performance of school children. The children will feel the impact of relocation or homelessness on their scholastic achievement because of the displacement from their homes and neighborhoods, as well as the financial and economic stresses (Moen, 1979); these children will inevitably encounter traumatic and distressing conditions by having to change schools at such times and by losing their friends. Further, they might have to share a room with other family members after having their own rooms or even have to move to a shelter. These emotional and physical events might cause nightmares, enuresis, or intrusive thoughts, depending on the age of the child. Adolescents in the family might move out of the house to go and fend for themselves. Lashley et al. (2009) posited that the Mortgage Bankers Association indicated one child in every American classroom is at risk of losing his or her home because the parents are unable to pay their mortgage. Galuszka (2008) further explained that minority students would have a particularly difficult time gaining access to colleges because those institutions are cutting their budgets and minority students might have problems obtaining student loans. At historically black schools, 70–80 percent of prospective students are eligible for Pell Grants because of their low income. These individuals will have to take on extra jobs to catch up. According to Galuszka, families confronted with foreclosures who have children attending private schools might have to decide between paying the mortgage or the tuition. Another direct impact of foreclosures on schoolchildren is the decline in their academic performance. Several researchers and publications (Butler, 2008; "Educating the Homeless," 2008) noted schoolchildren who frequently change locations are more likely to perform poorly academically and lose academic progress.

The third possible outcome of stress associated with foreclosure is widespread foreclosures also have an indirect impact on schoolchildren. Reduction of school funding results directly from less property tax revenue collected when homeowners do not pay the tax because of foreclosures. Because of less funding from the state, school leaders rethink their budgets to reflect current realities, and these cutbacks often involve personnel recruitment, staffing, and professional development.

The fourth possible outcome of stress associated with foreclosure is the primary breadwinner in the family might feel a reduction in his or her status in the community. A foreclosure can limit economic resources and disrupt the family system. Affected families might need to move from well-maintained communities to less affluent neighborhoods, leading to feelings of fear, disbelief, anxiety, hopelessness, and distress. Furthermore, Riley and Eckenrode (1986) noted stress might also affect extended family members and friends of families directly involved in the foreclosure and undergoing fiscal stress. A survey conducted by researchers at Freddie Mac/Roper of over 2,000 U.S. homeowner households in 2005 indicated approximately 60 percent of individuals delinquent on their mortgages are unaware of the assistance mortgage lenders can offer to distressed homeowners. The impact of foreclosures on the community's health could be significant because it affects the individual's and the family's health (Phillips, Clark, Lee, & Desautels, 2010). The effects on the local population include crime, loss of city revenue, disruption of social networks, and increases in blight.

Impact on Individual or Household Health

Individuals and families who experience high levels of stress resulting from foreclosures might have a host of physical and mental illnesses, causing damage to bodily systems, generating chronic health problems, and undermining their mental and emotional well-being (Pollack & Lynch, 2009). According to Renzetti and Edleson (2008), people currently experiencing impaired health who are undergoing the tension of foreclosure might find their preexisting conditions exacerbated, and the situation might trigger other harmful habits such as alcoholism and smoking. Financial stress might also contribute significantly to domestic violence (Renzetti & Edleson, 2008). Foreclosure might affect a person's credit and ability to maintain stable housing, thereby necessitating a decline into substandard living conditions that could affect health (Phillips et al., 2010).

Individuals in foreclosure must make sacrifices by choosing between taking care of their own health issues or finances. These decisions might include skipping or delaying meals, ignoring preventative health care measures, foregoing health insurance, or neglecting to maintain prescriptions and utility payments. Other family misfortunes include economic hardship and financial insecurity, displacement and housing instability, personal and family strain, broken relationships, compromised health, and adversity for children, the older adults, and renters. Pettit et al. (2009) noted a family's removal from home and the residential instability that follows might initiate a downward spiral that could prompt the family to seek assistance from a homeless shelter. Many families troubled by foreclosures might become homeless after moving into rental units, sharing space with family and friends, or seeking assistance from homeless shelters. Pettit et al. further noted sharing space with friends or family usually precedes homelessness.

Researchers at the National Coalition for the Homeless (2009) discovered poverty and homelessness are inevitably linked because impoverished families are often unable to pay for health care, education, housing, or food. Needy families often must make very difficult choices about how to use their limited available resources, and they might simply drop housing. In 2007, about 12.5 percent of the U.S. population (approximately 37,300,000 people) existed in destitution. A person caught in such circumstances is often one paycheck away from abject ruin and a life on the streets, which might occur after an illness or accident. The researchers at the National Coalition for the Homeless explained that two factors account for poverty: declining job opportunities and diminishing availability of public assistance. The limited availability of affordable housing and reduced number of housing assistance programs worsened the housing crisis and increased the incidence of homelessness. The unavailability of housing and its consequent high rent burdens have not only put a number of people at risk of homelessness but have forced many homeowners to become homeless.

Factors that might escalate homelessness include the lack of low-cost housing, poverty, lack of affordable health care, addiction disorders, domestic violence, and mental illness. Workers in the agricultural or service sectors tend to have limited work-based health insurance because health insurance provisions by employers have become more rare in recent years (Families USA, 2009). Tenants may become homeless quickly when they struggle to pay their rent because of serious illness or disability; the same is true for those with addiction problems. Job loss and depletion of savings normally precede eviction. Domestic violence and abusive relationships can also cause homelessness. The U.S. Conference of Mayors (2005) posited that domestic violence was the leading agent of homelessness from 50 percent of the cities surveyed. Further, many individuals with mental illness who receive appropriate supportive housing options can live successfully in a community (Center for Mental Health Services, 2003); the challenge is that obtaining access to these housing options and treatment services for mentally ill homeless people might be difficult. Without the appropriate treatment options for these differing groups of homeless people, it might be impossible for them to obtain housing as well as health care and recovery supports once on the streets.

Jayasundera, Silver, Anacker, and Mantcheva (2010) raised the issues concerning financial insecurity and economic hardship affecting homeowners struggling with their mortgages. Nonprofit organizations certified by the U.S. Department of Housing and Urban Development help homeowners prevent foreclosures with mitigation strategies. Approved counselors are loan resolution experts who seek equitable solutions on behalf of these families.

Foreclosures affect personal and family stress levels, disrupt relationships, and escalate ill health (Bennett, Scharoun-Lee, & Tucker-Seeley, 2009). Such potential health dangers, which are often of prolonged duration, have not gained much attention from policy makers worldwide, even though these same leaders have rushed to counter the economic impacts of the foreclosure crisis. Few if any researchers have reported specific disease consequences of home foreclosures or suggested foreclosure might increase the risk of chronic illness because the foreclosures might link to a possible range of health and psychological outcomes (Bennett et al., 2009). Policies intended to manage delinquencies and prevent foreclosures might protect those with the greatest health risk (Bennett et al., 2009).

Bennett et al. (2009) noted home foreclosures could be a stressor because of the aversive procedures and length of the process. U.S. banks usually retain all the home sale proceeds, whereas other nations, such as the United Kingdom, return net profits (once all debts are paid) to the foreclosed homeowner. The stress to families begins when they become delinquent on their mortgage and the bank starts the foreclosure process; the process itself varies substantially among different jurisdictions of the United States, ranging from several months to over a year (Immergluck, 2007; Schuetz, Been, & Ellen, 2008) and may include judicial supervision (Pence, 2006). Home foreclosures have phases of intensity through the process and can be stressful life events (Brown & Harris, 1978).

Indeed, previous studies have already listed foreclosure as one of the forty-three most stressful occurrences facing people in their lives. Foreclosure reached number 21 using the Social Readjustment Rating Scale in 1967 (Holmes & Rahe, 1967); by 1997, a study update revealed foreclosure had reached number 11 of such life happenings (Scully, Tosi, & Banning, 2000). It remains unclear how to explain independent effects of foreclosures, but Lazarus and Folkman (1984) suspected anxiety resulting from foreclosure surpassed families' ability to cope. Schneiderman, Ironson, and Siegel (2005) indicated foreclosure might influence psychological activity and behavior, as well as increase the chance of some chronic ailments such as cardiovascular disease. This implies a negative psychological impact of foreclosures on families.

Some possible psychological reactions to home foreclosures are important. According to Faravelli and Pallanti (1989) and Kendler, Gardner, and Prescott (2003), the etiology of anxiety and depression has implicated stressful life events. Strong evidence indicates disturbing life occurrences causally relate to the process and intensity of a foreclosure and the initial episode of depression (Finlay-Jones & Brown, 1981; Kendler, Karkowski, & Prescott, 1998). Chronic tension-producing agents such as job or financial stress often increase the effect of catastrophic life occurrences on depression, especially if the exposure of both stressors is simultaneous. Home foreclosure usually happens during prolonged financial crises in families and produces damaging health problems because of the tie to chronic stressors (Belkic, Landsbergis, Schnall, & Baker, 2004; Bosma, Peter, Siegrist, & Marmot, 1998; Dooley, Fielding, & Levi, 1996; Gallo, Bradley, Siegel, & Kasl, 2000; Grossi, Perski, Lundberg, &Soares, 2001; Shortt, 1996; Weich & Lewis, 1998). Several studies included examples of this association of depressive symptoms with chronic financial strain in populations from the United States, Britain, and China (Krause, 1987; Krause, Liang, & Gu, 1998).

Individuals become depressed when they feel some responsibility for a stressful life situation, and this might be common among people who experience foreclosures, despite the widely acknowledged notion that deceptive mortgage industry practices are to blame rather than solely the families (Schroeder, 2006). Individuals or families in the foreclosure process have limited control over the events surrounding them, and their sense of helplessness may increase the effect of stress on their depression (Benassi, Sweeney, & Dufour, 1988; Nettleton & Burrows, 2001). People with depression frequently demonstrate negative behaviors that can promote additional unfavorable life events, including job and financial problems and interpersonal conflicts (Hammen, 2006). Home foreclosures might affect health-related behaviors; clearly, unhealthy choices such as smoking, drinking alcohol, developing sleep disorders, and gaining weight are positively related to such stressful life events as foreclosures (Korkeila, Kaprio, Rissanen, Koshenvuo, & Sörensen, 1998).

Home foreclosures might also affect health care use; for example, financially distressed individuals might forgo preventive visits to physicians, reduce compliance to their prescription medication regimens, and switch from prescription drugs to over-the-counter drugs (Cobaugh et al., 2008). Both compositional and contextual dimensions are associated with susceptibility to home foreclosures. Cobaugh et al. (2008) noted individuals from minority ethnic backgrounds and with lower socioeconomic status might be particularly vulnerable and likely to experience stress and depression, as well as have limited opportunities to seek stress-buffering resources.

Many people who experience stressful life events are sufficiently resilient to get through them, but notable exceptions might exist for people with poor psychiatric and health histories, low self-esteem, poor coping mechanisms, inadequate social support systems, and emotional disturbance, as well as for those who highly value economic success, making them particularly vulnerable (Bleich, Gelkopf, & Solomon, 2003; Moos, Brennan, Schutte, & Moos, 2006). Soaring food, energy, and health care costs put financial strain on the average household, and coupled with the macroeconomic climate and detrimental contextual circumstances in times of economic uncertainties, those suffering through foreclosure might undergo increased stress exposure (Joint Center for Housing Studies of Harvard University, 2008). Unemployment seems to be the most troubling problematic macro-economic indicator, and combined with foreclosure in the present economic climate, the lack of a job appears particularly deleterious (Cahill, 1983; Colledge, 1982; Kasl, 1982).

According to Seifert (2005), more than 27 percent of those facing medical debt experienced some form of housing problem or insecurity as well, including the inability to make mortgage payments or qualify for a mortgage, difficulties paying rent, and the possibility of facing eviction. Many Americans are encountering rising health care costs and diminishing coverage, and millions have joined the ranks of the under-insured and uninsured, leaving a number of families facing health care costs they cannot manage (Families USA, 2009). This trend may lead more people deeper into debt, bankruptcy, and possible home foreclosure. Foreclosures cause individuals to become depressed and anxious, which are emotional states affecting marriages and relationships. In the face of foreclosure, people feel involved in a catastrophe, which leads to depression. Other effects include outbursts at work; an increase in drinking, abuse, and violence toward children; and suicide rates increasing (Armour, 2008).

Impacts on Children

Kachura (2011) posited that a multitude of factors might affect a city's housing market; two of the most significant of these problems are foreclosures and abandoned homes, which always cause a decline in the value of the house; then the foreclosures endanger families through loss of household wealth and neighborhood instability. Foreclosures directly affected nearly 3 percent of Baltimore City's students, as a representative example, and an additional 21 percent of the students affected by foreclosures move on to a new address the following year. According to Been, Ellen, Schwartz, Stiefel, and Weinstein (2010), many schools with large numbers of children whose families face foreclosure have the following characteristics: a larger degree of students receiving free or reduced-price lunches, a higher percentage of black students, and a smaller prevalence of students making adequate scores on standardized math and reading tests.

Been et al. (2010) noted housing instability could affect a child's academic ability in at least five areas: moving residences and sometimes doubling up with other family members, moving to different neighborhoods, stress for students causing anxiety or depression, moving to unfamiliar schools and falling behind or encountering conflict with classmates, and spillover effects on other children who may not have experienced foreclosures themselves. Disruption is an expectation for students with families undergoing housing instability when they move unexpectedly. Goux and Maurin (2005) and Maxwell (2003) have noted it is common for families experiencing foreclosure to take up residence with friends or end up homeless. Children's social networks might experience confusion because families must move from their neighborhoods as a result of foreclosure (Gruman, Harachi, Abbott, Catalano, & Fleming, 2008; South, Haynie, & Bose, 2007). Because of instability, students might have to change schools, possibly in the middle of the school year. According to Alexander, Entwisle, and Dauber (1996), as well as Lash and Kirkpatrick (1994), it appears that moving to new schools carries the possibility of causing problems related to achieving satisfactory scholastic performance.

One particularly significant factor is that students and their families might experience stress or trauma as a result of their housing uncertainty. These reactions might cause depression and more absences, as well as impair the students' ability to focus (Kingsley et al., 2009). The trauma of foreclosure makes relocating abruptly displaced children more difficult than it would have been if other happier circumstances precipitated the move. Children whose families remain unaffected by housing instability might suffer the spillover effects of affected children that slow the pace of their class (Hanushek, Kain, & Rivkin, 2004; Mehana & Reynolds, 2004). Calvó-Armengol, Patacchini, and Zenou (2009), Lavy and Schlosser (2011), and Weinberg (2007) indicated another consequence is exposure to crime and disorder in a high foreclosure community with an effect on the educational performance of children involved in foreclosure as well as their classmates. Equally important is the racial composition of the children whose families go through the foreclosure process. Been et al. (2010) disclosed that even though African American children accounted for 33 percent of those in the New York public schools in 2006 and 2007, they accounted for 57 percent of students living under the burden of foreclosure.

Lovell and Isaacs (2008) noted the impact of foreclosure on children and described such debilitating effects as disrupting their education; peer relationships; social networks; and most important their physical, emotional, and mental health. These outcomes remain essentially unintended, even unnoticed, until the chaos of the foreclosure crisis brings out behavioral issues in the affected children. Researchers at the Center for Responsible Lending (2007) estimated that in 2006, the number of struggling homeowners who had purchased their houses with subprime loans and would face foreclosure would reach 2.4 million, which would also affect their children. Lovell and Isaacs indicated the estimated number of children affected by race/ethnicity in the various households included 62 percent of owner-occupied Latino families with unsettled mortgages and an average of 2.08 youngsters with 504,600 children directly affected by the foreclosure crisis. The foreclosure crisis affected more than 281,000 African American children and 1.17 million white/other children. The foreclosure crisis could have directly affected 1.952 million young people.

A child's long-term chances of success with his or her education, health, and economic well-being rely on a host of components, including housing stability. The members of Partnership for America's Economic Success noted the high school graduation rate is far less for children who experience frequent moves in their early years (Partnership for America's Economic Success, 2008). Pettit (2004) further noted youngsters who move more frequently might seem disadvantaged compared to their unaffected counterparts, and such circumstances lead to reduced levels of employment capacity in early adulthood, a heightened probability of dropping out of high school, and decreased academic achievement.

Turbulence and instability have debilitating effects on children. Moore, Vandivere, and Ehrle (2000) defined experiencing turbulence as being a schoolchild who has moved from one state to another or changed schools during a twelve-month period. Turbulence may be short-lived or long-lived with its concurrent short-term or long-term risks to the child's development. Several indicators indicated turbulence might be higher in poor families than in more affluent families. More often, it appears that turbulence and instability occur with increased behavioral and emotional issues among children.

In the United States, an average of 6 percent of children experienced some form of turbulence, which doubled to 13 percent for children with family incomes below the federal poverty level (Moore et al., 2000). Addy, Engelhardt, and Skinner (2013) identified that 45 percent of children under the age of 18 live in low-income families, and 22 percent of these youngsters lived in poor families. The percentage increases significantly for families receiving federal or state assistance and food stamps and for children living with an unmarried parent or with parents who have not completed high school. A link might exist between turbulence and poorer outcomes for children, including raised levels of behavioral and emotional distress, reduced degrees of school involvement, more frequent suspension and expulsion, and higher instances of skipping school (Moore et al., 2000).

Impacts on Older Adults

Apgar (2008) explained the foreclosure crisis has had serious consequences on older adults. A sizable number of homeowners still have mortgages when they retire, which became evident in a study indicating that in 2007 over half of all breadwinner homeowners over age 50 maintained a mortgage, whereas only one-third of them were in that situation in 1987. It appears housing wealth continues to be a significant part of a financial buffer for seniors. In 2007, approximately 2.3 million elderly Americans had less than 20 percent equity in their homes. The significance of these numbers is that a decrease in home equity might hinder retirement and economic plans for these elderly Americans.

The housing market downturn and the stock market plunge adversely affected many retirees in their foremost means of income because their homes and investments were their primary assets (Green, 2008). Many retirees struggled economically and sought jobs. Another problem for retirees as a result of the housing crisis is difficulty selling their houses to move into assisted-living centers or retirement communities (Healy, 2008). Unsold houses or condominiums for these people make it practically impossible to afford the payment to buy into retirement homes because they may have to pay $100,000 to $500,000 to relocate.

Shelton (2008) revealed older African Americans and Hispanics have higher foreclosure rates than their Caucasian counterparts of any age. Older Americans in general have less time and ability to recover from a financial crisis, and resulting losses from home foreclosures jeopardize their finances. The prospect of moving to a different environment is especially difficult for older individuals (Smith & Ferryman, 2006) and might be more difficult when it results from problematic conditions such as foreclosure. Older residents might have lived in their home for much of their lives and might have raised their children there. Rowles (1983, 1993) noted the comfortable old neighborhood provides a connection to social networks and familiarity with neighbors and offers a personal sense of belonging. Even if these seniors must involuntary move from blighted communities to somewhat better ones, they might still experience grim outcomes with respect to health, social support, and personal mobility (Danermark & Ekström, 1990). Relocation of seniors might exacerbate their chronic conditions if their health is already poor and precipitate mental stress over moving from their homes, neighbors, and familiar surroundings. Keith (1993) also studied the vulnerability of older adults when exposed to chronic financial strain and found both older men and older women would lose their sense of control and become distressed when exposed to financial difficulties.

Impacts on Renters

The foreclosure crunch also significantly affected renters, and affected tenants have become the victims of problems they did not create. According to Treves (2011), in 2010, tenants had to endure banks' policies of evicting all tenants of foreclosed properties, resulting in needless displacement of families and leaving neighborhoods with abandoned homes and blighted conditions. Treves noticed that attempts at persuading mortgage companies to keep renting to their tenants have failed, and the banks persist in the wholesale eviction of all occupants. The potential loss to banks is staggering because the rental income they forfeited was approximately $755 million in 2010. Other costs to banks include paying lawyers to handle eviction cases as well as paying realtors to negotiate their cash-for-keys deals. Vacant buildings cause property values in the community to decrease, led the buildings to become targets for vandalism, and generate legal liability for banks as the owners of blighted abandoned property. Bankers' insistence on evicting innocent tenants diminished their reputation in the local area.

Treves (2011) observed many tenants find out that they are in foreclosure only when they face imminent displacement. Foreclosure can damage a tenant's life in a number of ways; for example, preforeclosure tenants might face health hazards because their defaulting landlords ignore their requests for maintenance and allow the structures to deteriorate. Habitability worsens after a foreclosure when a bank assumes ownership of a property; that is, the property becomes real estate owned. At that point, the banks might evict and displace tenants and many might struggle to find alternative housing. Some may not receive their security deposits back. Other problems involve living far from their workplaces and schools for their children and social networks, and still other tenants may become homeless. Some tenants have experienced displacement from multiple houses because more than one landlord defaulted on mortgages, even when the tenants paid rent on time. Such situations undermine housing stability and become damaging to the elderly, individuals with disabilities, and families with children.

Some researchers ("Foreclosures," 2013) observed that a 61 percent rise in homelessness occurred in 2008 according to state and local homeless groups. The laws in most areas lack adequate protections for people living in homes caught in the foreclosure process (National Law Center on Homelessness and Poverty [NLCHP], 2010). The only two areas of the country that provide limited protection in terms of lease survival issues are New Jersey and the District of Columbia. Tenants living in foreclosed properties in at least three states could be subject to eviction proceedings to vacate the property after three days' notice.

Treves (2010) noted unscrupulous behavior from private investors and banks that acquire properties at foreclosure continues to plague the nation, despite the adoption and expansion of tenant protection laws. Banks and investors contract with eviction law firms and real estate agents to deceive and harass tenants in foreclosure situations to vacate and sell their foreclosed properties. Realtors see the tenants as obstacles to obtaining their commission checks after selling foreclosed properties, so they employ scare tactics and offer misinformation and cash incentives provided by the banks and investors to induce tenants to move out quickly. However, tenants lose their legal rights when signing such agreements to vacate their homes (Treves, 2010). Eviction law firm professionals violate tenant rights by filing eviction lawsuits against those living in foreclosed homes. The affected tenants might avoid fighting these wrongful lawsuits for fear of risking their strong tenant history and giving the appearance of being a defendant in an eviction case, because of a lack of knowledge of their tenant rights, or due to their inability to afford legal representation (Treves, 2011).

Researchers at Tenants Together (2009) noted the impact of foreclosure on tenants was as follows:

1. Evicted through no fault of their own
2. Denied information about what is going on with their homes
3. Evicted without receiving sixty-day notice
4. Forced to live without water, gas, or electricity
5. Cannot reach owners to get repairs done
6. Losing their security deposits
7. Subject to rent skimming
8. Victims of fraud and deceptive practices
9. Credit damaged
10. Unable to get legal services
11. Forced into homelessness

Evicted through no fault of their own. Even though landlords generally inactivate leases following a foreclosure, the law entitles renters to sixty days' written notice to vacate the premises. Most tenants will face eviction attempts after foreclosure sales, despite protective laws in certain cities such as certain just-cause-for-eviction laws and ninety-day notices of termination for Section 8 renters. Most renters face eviction from foreclosed properties because of bank policies to prepare vacated buildings for sale quickly.

The state of California enacted just-cause-for-eviction laws in some cities in California, which stipulate that a landlord must have a reasonable cause for removing a tenant, and foreclosure is not one of the reasons authorized. Representatives of banks and mortgage companies, as well as their real estate agents, continue to evict tenants and violate local just-cause ordinances, even though such actions could lead to civil or criminal lawsuits. Bank representatives and their realtors unlawfully remove many Section 8 tenants entitled to a ninety-day notice (Tenants Together, 2009). Low-income tenants need protecting, and displacing Section 8 renters conflicts with the housing assistance contracts signed to protect this group.

Denied information about what is going on with their homes. Banks do not have to serve default notices upon tenants, but banks must serve notices of sale upon renters twenty days prior to the sale of the residence, which provides renters an opportunity to prepare to moving out if asked to do so. Tenants might be the last to know of an impending foreclosure sale. Because the banks do not have to serve the notice of default but are only required to serve the notice of trustee sale twenty days before the foreclosure sale, which creates panic in the affected individuals because of the limited time to make moving and housing decisions (Tenants Together, 2009). Treves (2011) also corroborated in his research that tenants do not receive information about the foreclosure status of their rental properties until the last minute when they face displacement.

Evicted without receiving sixty-day notice. The current legal environment favors the banks by not enforcing the laws requiring a sixty-day notice of their intention to evict tenants. Bank's attorneys may serve eviction lawsuits upon renters, or the sheriff might show up to forcibly evict all the residents, whether renters or owners. Tenants might live in misrepresented owner-occupied properties because the banks might have improperly proceeded with nonexistent owner occupants, which caused displacement to the true renter occupants (Tenants Together, 2009).

Forced to live without water, gas, or electricity. Defaulting property owners might not pay for utilities such as water, gas, and electricity when facing foreclosure or the foreclosing bank might refuse to pay for such services to force tenants to move out. Landlords or foreclosing banks performing such acts may be illegal, and the tenants must be given the opportunity to transfer such utility services to their own names without the prior liability of the previous owner. There could be serious health and safety repercussions for these tenants, especially those who are the most at risk: older adults and families with children. With no utilities and housing services, these tenants must move out (Tenants Together, 2009). Tenants in a preforeclosure situation face serious health hazards because their defaulting landlords often failed to maintain the property; they could find themselves without utilities (Treves, 2011). This is particularly true when the property is foreclosed, a situation that could be especially traumatic for seniors, families with children, and tenants with disabilities.

Cannot reach owners to get repairs done. Defaulting homeowners frequently neglect rental properties, even though the law requires that they maintain basic habitability standards and notify tenants about who is responsible for managing the property. When ownership changes, the law prescribes that the new management inform tenants of the new property manager's name within fifteen days. Defaulting homeowners are often unreachable when tenants need them on requests for repairs, which causes renters to exist in substandard conditions or pay for repairs that the homeowner is responsible for handling. After a foreclosure sale, the problem worsens because the banks are extremely unresponsive to the needs of the tenants because the banks are eager for them to move so they can prepare the property for sale (Tenants Together, 2009).

Losing their security deposits. Tenants living in a foreclosed property and having to vacate the premises often lose their security deposits even though property owners are required to return them within three weeks or to properly document any deductions from those deposits. When the property is foreclosed, these renters have the right to receive their security deposits once they are asked or forced to move out; however, the banks or new owners normally ignore these rights and simply keep the deposit. It appears that tenants who may be in full compliance with the terms of their lease may be unable to recover their security deposits when they are forced to vacate their housing through foreclosure (NLCHP, 2010). This could be particularly perilous for lower-income tenants who need to access safe and affordable housing to avoid homelessness.Of course, the tenants would be better served if they received their security deposits back because they could use these funds toward their new housing costs (Tenants Together, 2009).

Subject to rent skimming. Rent skimming occurs when landlords collect rent and fail to pay the mortgage during the first year of their ownership of the property. This situation puts tenants at risk of a foreclosure sale and subsequent eviction because of the irresponsible behaviors of their landlords when they default. This situation undermines tenants' rights to stay in the property because they have paid their rents dutifully. Current laws often prohibit deceptive business practices and fraud; nevertheless, tenants are still victims of these acts. Further, some people commit various scams on tenants during the foreclosure process, some of which are criminal offences. Some individuals may present themselves to unsuspecting tenants as the owners of the property and charge them hefty security deposits as well as first and last month's rent. The tenants then discover they have no right to live on the property (Tenants Together, 2009).

Victims of fraud and deceptive practices. Defaulting landlords might continue to collect rent from tenants even after the foreclosure sale. After that sale takes place, the foreclosed homeowner has no right to collect rents but is a common practice because the landlord threatens tenants with eviction when they refuse to pay. Another deceptive practice by landlords is failing to disclose an imminent foreclosure to a prospective tenant. Tenants enter leases and pay security deposits, but when a foreclosure terminates the leases, tenants lose their security deposits and face possible eviction by the new landlord (Tenants Together, 2009).

Credit damaged. Damaged credit is a serious financial setback for most people, and a tenant with an eviction lawsuit history might find it difficult to acquire new housing. Tenants who contest foreclosure evictions in a court might avoid showing the eviction record after they win the case within the sixty days after the court seals this record. Other tenants might find it challenging to secure new housing after losing a foreclosure eviction case and with its appearance on their credit reports (Tenants Together, 2009).

Unable to get legal services. Because landlord-tenant law is extremely complicated and highly specialized, tenants without legal representation are at a disadvantage against their landlords who do have such representation regarding eviction cases. The difficulty of maneuvering through the legal system intensifies for seniors, individuals with limited English proficiency, those who may be ill, and tenants with other disabilities. If tenants cannot assert their legal rights in court, protective laws have little effect. According to researchers at the National Low Income Housing Coalition (2009), legal service agencies are understandably overwhelmed with requests for assistance from tenants in foreclosed properties. The researchers further noted maintaining or losing housing depends to a great extent on access to legal assistance and added that government funding to these service agencies to provide their training and information sharing on rights is critical to assisting tenants in this situation. Fireside (2009) contended the Obama administration's mortgage rescue plan nearly overlooked the needs of tenants in foreclosure who have little knowledge of their legal rights. Community organizers and certain legal advocates are trying to help bring equity to the plight of these forgotten people by pressuring policy makers, lenders, and the legal system.

Forced into homelessness. Foreclosure sale evictions are causing many tenants to end up homeless, including children, the elderly, and individuals with disabilities. Sometimes abandoned property continues to lie vacant while tenants wind up in temporary shelters or living in alleys or under bridges. The loss of security deposits, inadequate timing of the eviction notice, and credit report damage, all of which make it difficult to secure new housing, exacerbate the problems they experience (White, 2009). People can avoid the trauma of homelessness, which can cause lifelong harm, especially to children, by preventing homelessness in the first place, which is a strategy that makes moral, practical, and financial sense (NLCHP, 2009). Preventing homelessness will avoid disruption to community, school, and work ties among families.

Impacts on Neighborhoods. Treuhaft, Kalima, and Black (2010) posited that the housing and mortgage crisis has strongly affected low-income groups, and subprime mortgages strongly affected people with ethnic backgrounds. According to a recent analysis conducted at UCLA, the greatest loss of wealth for Latinos and African Americans in modern times included an estimated $200 billion squandered to foreclosures since 2007 (Ojeda, Jacquez, & Takash, 2009). Personal wealth is consumed for the low-income community of Latinos and African Americans where foreclosures are normally concentrated.

Declining property values, physical deterioration. Treuhaft et al. (2010) indicated many low-income neighborhoods affected by foreclosures need investment to avoid deterioration of the area and to revitalize the community. Plummeting property values in these affected neighborhoods are significant. Approximately 70 million neighborhood homes have lost $150 billion in value. Foreclosed properties cause those nearby to lose between 0.6 and 1.6 percent, or an average of $7,200 of a home's value. A major part of this problem results from investor ownership, which can cause a significant decrease in home values that might result from the business model adopted to make a profit in low- to moderate-income neighborhoods.

Foreclosed properties might become vacant and might have wider implications for the finances of the city or county ("Communities at Risk," 2009). These issues are particularly strong in areas where the homeowners owe more than the value of the property. In these neighborhoods, physical decay and abandonment take place quickly, and these markets are in the weak market regions where housing prices are already relatively low. Maintenance by either the bank or the new investor-owner becomes a problem because of the slim prospect of resale. Thieves move in quickly to steal copper wires, pipes, and fixtures within days of the property's vacancy. The effect is that the property decays, causing neighboring property values to decrease as well. Selling off abandoned or vacant properties in strong housing markets takes place faster because of equity in the property. Absentee investor-owners usually ignore maintaining these properties and end up showing symptoms of the weaker markets (Treuhaft et al., 2010).

Emerging trends and reports confirm that some areas of Queens, New York, are similar to Cleveland or Detroit where bank-owned properties fail to sell, thieves steal copper stripping and anything they believe they can resell, arson happens, and drug dealers and squatters move in (Wisloski, 2008). Some cities and counties have a mix of weak and strong housing markets, with some areas showing healthy demand and others having weak demand.

Crime, social disorder, population turnover. The mortgage crisis has led to many lessons for many stakeholders, and one lesson applicable to banks and mortgage lenders is evictions (Miroff, 2008). Before evictions, homeowners or renters receive two warning letters and then sheriffs forcefully remove them from the property on the day of the eviction. Evictions can cause displacement and changes in a community's population. Problems that might happen after an eviction include leaking water heaters that destroy carpets and flooring, messy cabinets, and stolen property like copper wiring.

Mummolo and Brubaker (2008) noted that when a foreclosed home becomes vacant, crime follows immediately. Vacant properties become a safe haven for squatters, vandals, thieves, prostitutes, drug users, or teenagers' intent on partying. Frustrated and former home-owners may also engage in illegal activities such as stripping their houses of toilets, stoves, refrigerators, air conditioners, and even hardwood floors before leaving the property. Evicted and foreclosed residents have become angry and performed actions that may be criminal as a demonstration of defiance to the foreclosing bank.

Local government fiscal stress and deterioration of services. Foreclosure increases costs for cities and counties with regard to maintaining and securing vacant properties, following up calls on police and fire issues, pursuing court actions, and carrying out demolitions ("Communities at Risk," 2009). Cities spend between $430 and $34,000 on each abandoned property. Further, school budgets might decrease because of limited revenue, and students would suffer. Schools might have to serve homeless children and manage these youngsters, who develop academic, behavioral, or delinquency problems as a result of the displacement of their families (Lovell & Isaacs, 2008).

Variations in impacts for different types of neighborhoods. As foreclosures continue to drain families' wealth, the situation affects communities of people of color (particularly African American and Latino homeowners) the hardest (Bocian, Li, & Ernst, 2010). Between 2007 and 2009, banks foreclosed on an estimated 2.5 million homes, and an additional 5.7 million homes were in danger of foreclosure. Seventeen percent of Black and 11 percent of Hispanic homeowners have experienced a foreclosure. The foreclosures mostly occurred on owner-occupied homes. One case study indicated the abundance and effects of predatory mortgage loans in rural regions of the United States according to data from the Home Mortgage Disclosure Act and share of subprime loans in rural as well as poor counties (Singleton, George, Dickstein, & Thomas, 2006).

Mallach (2008) noted the highest hit areas affected by foreclosure could apply some specific policy solutions or recommendations for a state, Ohio in particular, to stabilize its neighborhoods. Lenders might pay a foreclosure filing fee to fund foreclosure prevention counseling and neighborhood stabilization programs, bar abusive lending practices and surety bond requirements, and provide enforcement for mortgage brokers for states and local jurisdictions.

Determinants of foreclosure patterns. In an econometric analysis in the Washington DC area, Jayasundera et al. (2010) used 2004–2007 statistical samples of loans and noted Hispanics and African Americans obtained subprime, nontraditional loans more frequently than their white counterparts of similar neighborhoods and economic characteristics. Ethnic minority borrowers are undergoing foreclosures more frequently than white borrowers, even after acknowledging certain control measures. The loans purchased by government-sponsored enterprises perform better, with a rate of foreclosure half that of privately securitized loans and portfolio loans. Loan features such as subprime, payment-to-income ratios, balloon payments, and adjustable rates have negative effects on overall performance of loans.

Robinson and Todd (2010) investigated occupant and nonoccupant homeowner characteristics and observed lower credit risk and higher credit scores for nonoccupant homeowners, but when these individuals see the value of their houses fall, they may experience weaker incentives to keep up their mortgage payments. This effect occurred in Midwestern and Northeastern states, with a high rate of foreclosure per mortgage but not a high volume of mortgages. The worst situation occurred in Florida and Nevada, where nonoccupant owners experienced a high volume of mortgages as well as a high rate of foreclosure on those mortgages.

Impact on community health. Foreclosure affects community health and has direct ties to the individual effects of foreclosures. The displacement and relocation of families bring about the loss of their sense of fellowship in the community as well as the stabilizing social networks that previously uplifted them. Another significant effect is the deferment of property maintenance because these homeowners face decisions about incurring these expenses or leaving their homes, decreasing property values, and the consequent loss of city revenue (Furman Center, 2010). According to Phillips et al. (2010), vacant properties often fuel negative activities such as drugs and crime.

Coping mechanisms. Moen (1979) defined coping mechanisms as the behaviors that can assist in reducing the harmful effects of stress in general and of foreclosures in particular. One such strategy would be for people to locate alternate income and housing sources. This resource should be readily available to vulnerable individuals and families undergoing the social and emotional trauma of mortgage foreclosures. Victims of foreclosure should receive information concerning food pantries, shelters, and medical and psychological educational services, as well as financial assistance. Gray et al. (2004) noted such information would enable these individuals to cope with the trauma of their worsening situation as well as increase their knowledge to improve their decisions and choices. Effective communication among family members might help to solidify their relationships and might be especially helpful for failing relationships.

Modes of interventions. Early intervention is necessary to prevent chronic psychopathology and must be empirical. The following cognitive and behavioral strategies are important methods of intervention: social and familial support, grief counseling, and cognitive behavioral techniques (Lashley et al., 2009). One method of intervention, a type of social and familial support, includes educating family members to reduce stress by knowing various coping mechanisms. Openly discussing a foreclosure event might help relieve individuals of the stress associated with the initial shocks of the foreclosure. Family therapy is a means of reestablishing trust among family members, improving their communication, and redefining their relationships.

Lashley et al. (2009) recommended obtaining additional help for the primary wage earner in particular, because he or she might obsess over the loss and self-blame. Clinicians can measure the level of depression using the Beck Scale of Depression and verify whether any depression existed before the foreclosure to ensure a beneficial counseling outcome and level of treatment.

Using a cognitive behavioral approach might help a family gain a quality of self-worth and highlight strengths upon which family members can build. Decreasing the impulse to blame themselves might help to enable them to grow again (Lashley et al., 2009). Having the right attitude to thrive in the face of adversity is critical to coping with the stress associated with foreclosure. McEwen (2011) described resilience by offering such words as "bounce-back," "rebound," and "recoil" to elaborate on how resilient individuals respond to setbacks and obstacles in their lives (p. 2); whereas, Maddi and Khoshaba (2005) noted less resilient people show vulnerability under stress. The various attributes of resilience are the ability to challenge and control oneself, to possess a hardy attitude of commitment, to exhibit transformational coping skills, and to develop a two-way social support system. Such a support system would effectively center on the responses to and from family members. The authors asserted hardiness must be engrained in a resilient personality to successfully survive and thrive under stress; they further advised maintaining the attitudes of the 3 Cs: control, commitment, and challenge (p. 13). All these qualities were evident in a research study on people involved in losing their jobs with Illinois Bell Telephone, where Maddi and Khoshaba identified four traits in those who demonstrated exceptional coping skills: a person (a) thrives on change, (b) takes decisive action, (c) is resilient with family, and (d) is future oriented. Despite these efforts, unresolved health-related impacts of home foreclosures on affected people and families remain a concern and require further research.

According to Hartley (2010), Campbell, Giglio, and Pathak performed a study on the price of homes in Massachusetts and reported that a foreclosure sale is approximately 27 percent below comparable properties and decreases the selling prices of other houses within a distance of 260 feet by 1 percent. This information indicates 10 foreclosed properties in a neighborhood might reduce the sale price of a nonforeclosed property by 10 percent, which is a significant effect. Eggum et al. (2008) observed foreclosures continue to be more common than loan modification, even though the strategy is a favored means for reducing foreclosures. Eggum et al. (2008) noted, "Bankruptcy permits homeowners to halt foreclosures and cure defaults on their mortgage loans by repaying missed payments over a period of years. However, families face serious challenges in saving their homes using bankruptcy law.… Bankruptcy law does not permit debtors to modify the terms of mortgages secured by a principal residence." (p. 1125)

Eggum et al. also explained a crucial assumption is that persons involved with Chapter 13 bankruptcy have incomes that are sufficient and will allow them to make mortgage payments and cover additional living expenses, which are requirements to obtain a bankruptcy discharge. This is evident in the antimodification rule under the Bankruptcy Code that stipulates bankruptcy debtors may not adjust the terms of their home mortgages. General rules regarding the modification of claims in bankruptcy permit individuals to modify the rights of secured and unsecured creditors under U.S. Bankruptcy Code 11 U.S.C. §1322(b)(2). Changing the schedule of payments or reducing the contract interest rate can alter secured claims, but the restriction on loan changes sometimes makes it difficult for those with high mortgages to avoid foreclosure through bankruptcy.

Chapter 13 bankruptcy requirements for financially handicapped homeowners do not permit them to become better off or to aggrandize their lifestyle. Eggum et al. (2008) made clear that such families must live on a managed budget for three to five years, and if their income does not increase during that time, they will face fixed or increasing housing expenses that restrict their ability to manage unforeseen expenses. The Chapter 13 repayment plan might extend homeowners' financial adversity during the period and lengthen their financial suffering, only to lose the home to foreclosure after all.

Conclusions

Rollins (2003) noted not enough studies exist to elucidate the relationship between foreclosure and medical distress. The lack of stable housing and substandard living conditions for families caught in this disaster might negatively affect their health (Phillips et al., 2010). To ensure stability in the family system during events such as foreclosures, federal and state foreclosure task force must make concerted efforts to tackle the psychosocial needs of all affected individuals. Lashley et al. (2009) noted the trauma of foreclosure is comparable to large-scale catastrophes such as natural disasters and terrorism that inevitably lead to physical injuries, property damage, and even loss of life, followed immediately by significant emotional and psychological distress for those who survive. Lashley et al. further believed foreclosure victims face additional trauma in the sense that they continue to feel devastated by a sense of inadequacy, self-doubt, and overwhelming feelings of guilt. Appropriate research on social, psychological, and similar efforts should be pursued and instituted in suitable agencies to manage the severe anguish resulting from foreclosure to affected individuals and families

Summary

Research offers growing evidence of a connection between foreclosure and physical and mental illness in both individuals and families. According to Rohe and Stegman (1994) and Lubell, Crain, and Cohen (2007), while home ownership often relates to an agreeable sense of well-being, it might produce the reverse when individuals or families lose their homes through foreclosure. The foreclosure process can indeed be traumatic and stressful (Bennett et al., 2009). The study involved empirically linking foreclosures and their potentially negative effects to the health of family members.

CHAPTER 3

Methodology

The purpose of the qualitative phenomenological analysis was to examine the participant's lived experiences of the potentially deleterious consequences of home foreclosures on physical and mental health among people in northern New Jersey, using semistructured and transcribed interviews. The conclusions augmented the body of information on the debilitating physical and mental illness caused by home foreclosures on individuals and families and could help in policy responses to help struggling homeowners. This methodology and design chapter contains a description of the instrument used for the study, the methods of collecting the research data, the population, and the selection of questions. This chapter also includes the data analysis and validity of the study's findings.

Research Method

Through this project, the researcher addressed the potential negative influences of home foreclosures on the physical and mental health of residents in northern New Jersey using semistructured and transcribed interviews to evaluate the various coping mechanisms used by members of the families involved and to assess any available interventions. The project additionally ascertained whether some effects are more prevalent than others to encourage the appropriate policy responses. The analysis involved a qualitative research design, and the methodology used was a phenomenological approach that involved interviewing homeowners going through the foreclosure process. Balls (2009) posited the focus of phenomenology is the substance of living experience and consciousness that could include emotions, perceptions, and judgments.

According to Connelly (2010), a researcher taking a phenomenological approach to understand the experiences of study participants analyzes the importance or qualities of an experience through observations, interviews, or stories related by the research subjects. This method of inquiry, called *lived experience*, has a focus on the essence of experience from the point of view of the individual going through the situation. Two primary phenomenological approaches are common: *descriptive* (developed by Husserl) or *interpretive* (also called *hermeneutic*, developed by Heidegger). Jaromahum and Fowler (2010) explained the technique of bracketing as important to fit the purpose of the study. More specifically, descriptive researchers attempt to put aside, or bracket, the participants' biases to avoid their effects on the study whereas interpretive phenomenologists include them because they do not think they can ignore these biases, being an integral part of the person living the experience and a necessity for the researcher to analyze. The current study followed a descriptive approach. Armour, Rivaux, and Bell (2009) noted one important attribute of a phenomenological study is that sample sizes are frequently quite limited and purposeful so a researcher can profoundly immerse him or herself in the material and thus the phenomenon itself. The data consisted of the material gathered from the interviews with the people living the experience. Once collected, the researcher must spend substantial time with the information to comprehend the lived experience of the subjects in detail. To validate the findings of the study and ultimately to form some conclusions, the researcher combines pieces of data into themes and subthemes to compare them across interviews.

Research Design

The descriptive phenomenological method was suitable for this qualitative phenomenological study to obtain a deeper understanding of the individuals taking part in the project (Garson, 2002). The method supported the use of several data collection modes such as interviews, observation, and sensitive appraisal. According to Stein and Makowski (2004), four phases exist in a qualitative research analysis: the acts of witnessing, asking, knowing, and interpreting. These phases involve having direct knowledge of the research subjects, identifying the focus of inquiry, construing the collective experiences of the project's responders, and translating the conversations and interpretations of the participants into useful research products for a particular audience.

The present study includes answers to the following questions, which included a concentration on the health-related effects of foreclosures: (a) the self-reported medical consequences of foreclosures, (b) the consequences of medical insurance in foreclosures, and (c) the medical issues that account for the hospitalization of family members during foreclosures.

Particular attention went to the causes and consequences of a medical crisis that might mainly be physical and mental illness or injury to the individual him or herself as well as to the spouse or others in the family, medical bills, drug or alcohol abuse, gambling, and birth or death in the family.

Research Method and Design Appropriateness

The study involved adapting the qualitative phenomenological approach to gain knowledge of the phenomenon of living through potential physical and mental illnesses related to home foreclosures. According to Giorgi (1970), phenomenology refers to the phenomenon of consciousness and the totality of experiences lived by a person. Giorgi's descriptive phenomenological method with a clear structure was therefore suitable. Because the research involved the phenomenon of living through the foreclosure process, considerable research is necessary for a coherent and understandable portrayal of the experience (Connelly, 2010). The study conveyed the participants' experience clearly to its audience, making it possible to understand the perils related to foreclosure without enduring it themselves.

Population and Samples

The study involved investigating the possible pernicious consequences of home foreclosures on the mental and physical health of northern New Jersey homeowners. To achieve the goal of understanding this crisis, a sample of twenty-five homeowners in the process of foreclosure participated in interviews. The phenomenological approach made it possible for them to tell their own stories. Recruiting study participants involved obtaining a list of homeowners in the process of foreclosure from the free public websites http://www.realtytrac.com and http://www.corelogic.com for property and ownership information in the Essex and Union Counties of New Jersey. The researcher sent the potential participants the solicitation of volunteers request forms (see appendix A). Any interested volunteers over the age of 18 signed the informed consent agreement (see appendix B). After those agreeing to take part in the study scheduled a meeting at a convenient time, the researcher conducted the interview provided in Robinson et al.'s Mortgage Foreclosure Study (see appendix C).

Data Collection Procedures

An approach using observation and interview was suitable for the qualitative analysis. The format for the interviews was a telephone or in-person interaction between the researcher and the research volunteer. Interviewing in general has the advantage of being flexible, reaching a greater data depth, following up on clues for answers, and employing questions that are semistructured (Strauss & Myburgh, 2001). According to Strauss and Myburgh (2001), the main benefits of interviews, whether using structured or unstructured questions, are a more profound depth of the information received, improved flexibility with a higher percentage of responses provided, and the capacity to probe further for answers using follow-up questions.

Kuipers (1994) noted qualitative simulation involves locating all the consistent behaviors with the knowledge in the model, and qualitative models are capable of expressing the states of incomplete knowledge about a continuous mechanism more than traditional model. The investigation involved qualitative research inquiry to explain the experiences lived by the research participants.

Leedy and Ormrod (2010) suggested

> Using semi-structured interviews [ensures] that participants provide a fuller, richer account than would [be] possible with a standard quantitative instrument, allowing for considerable flexibility in probing interesting areas that emerge. Interviews are usually taped and transcribed verbatim and then subjected to detailed qualitative analysis—attempting to elicit key themes in the participant's speech. (p. 159)

An advantage of tape recording is that it involves capturing the whole interview and enables thoroughgoing and completely accurate analysis of the data. The participants' responses were tape-recorded.

The researcher advised the research participants of the interview's anticipated timeframe to help them plan accordingly. The researcher and the participant agreed upon a time to meet or call before the interview. The in-person interviews needed a public venue with few or no distractions. In addition, the participants provided written permission that allowed the researcher to quote the respondents. The participants received a copy of the informed consent form to sign before the interview sessions began (see appendix B). The interview resulted in an individual structural description, an individual textural description, and a textural or structural description of each participant's experience. Robertson et al. (2008) conducted the Mortgage Foreclosure Study (see appendix C). The permission to use an existing survey form appears in appendix D).

Withdrawal Process of Study Participants

The volunteers could withdraw even after the data collection was complete by calling or e-mailing the researcher. After receiving a withdrawal request, the researcher would have immediately removed any data collected from the individual either by deleting the soft copy of the coded or raw information or by shredding the hard copy of any material on that person to ensure security and confidentiality.

Confidentiality and Data Integrity

By law, as well as for the integrity of the data collected, researchers must maintain the confidentiality of all information pertaining to research participants. Only the University of Phoenix Institutional Review Board could have access to this information. Confidential information of participants can include names, characteristics, other identifying information, questionnaire scores, ratings, incidental comments, information accrued either directly or indirectly through contact with any individual, or any other information considered confidential.

To maintain the confidentiality of the study, disclosing any such material to an individual or entity who is not part of the actual research study or who required the information for the express purposes of the research program was not allowable. Confidentiality in this case included not having a conversation regarding the study or its participants in a place where any unauthorized person might overhear such a discussion. For data integrity reasons, all research records, whether paper, electronic, or otherwise, remained in a secured and supervised location. If the services of a third party must be used to assist in the development of the project, an agreement will be signed because of the potential to access the participants' confidential information to ensure the provision of the minimum confidential obligations set forth in this section. The researcher would have informed any known or suspected violations of this confidentiality statement regarding this research project to the Institutional Review Board of the University of Phoenix.

Instruments

The survey instrument contained open-ended questions. Other, more structured questions built upon on the validity of a comparable analysis conducted by Robertson et al. (2008) on the medical causes of home mortgage foreclosures. Adapting the instrument involved adding specific open-ended questions to facilitate the need to investigate and understand the possibly negative consequences of home foreclosures on physical and mental health. The Mortgage Foreclosure Study (see appendix C) was from Robertson et al. (2008). The permission to use an existing survey form also appears in appendix D. To assist in fully exploring the research questions, twenty-five homeowners in the process of foreclosure comprised the population interviewed using semistructured interviews. The modes of the interviews involved an in-person or telephonic format, and both were advantageous in gathering information. According to Strauss and Myburgh (2001), the main benefits of interviews, whether using structured or unstructured questions, include a more profound depth of the information received, flexibility with a higher percentage of responses provided, and the capacity to probe further for answers on follow-up questions.

Face-to-face interviews. Participants in the face-to-face format participated in one-to-one interviews with the researcher. According to Carey and Durant (2000), this format allows for probing and clarification of responses from open-ended questions. Saunders, Lewis, and Thornhill (2003) indicated a semistructured interview is an effective approach for probing the issues more thoroughly and effectively than structured and standardized interviews. Semistructured interviews do not restrict the answers of research participants. The disadvantages of in-person interviewing include time and cost, especially if the interviewers are receiving pay; sensitive issues are more difficult to address when people are sitting face-to-face than when they respond in a written questionnaire format; and accidentally influencing answers by a verbal or physical cue or action of the interviewer. The study participants were unpaid volunteers.

Telephone interviews. One interview took place over the telephone instead of face-to-face. According to Irvine (2011), telephone interviews require less time and money without needing to travel to and from the participants' locations. Telephone interviews allow a study to include more people on a wider geographical scale as well as provide access to persons in unsafe or potentially dangerous environments. Benefits of an ethical nature include greater anonymity and less intensity afforded by a telephone interview, which are considerations that might be preferable for topics of a sensitive nature to research participants (Chapple, 1999). Most interviews took between twenty-five and thirty minutes.

Gerson and Horowitz (2002) mentioned some disadvantages of telephone interviews, such as the difficulty of establishing rapport with the subjects because of missing their nonverbal reactions and cues not witnessed and investigated. Participants on a telephone interview may not take much time to think about their responses, and that sense of distance and rush might produce inaccurate findings.

Validity

When designing a research questionnaire, researchers must collect appropriate valid information. The study included an existing questionnaire modified with the addition of specific health-related questions administered through interviews.

Creswell (2009) noted that the validity of a qualitative phenomenological study depends on the researcher accurately depicting the data. When the study design affords accurate results, then the study is internally valid.

Accreditation of the data describes the use of the content and data in the study (Gioia, Corley, & Hamilton, 2013), which helps explain the entire theme of the study, along with its details, properly and effectively. This accreditation of the data assists in the development of a set of effective recommendations, which the researcher then practically applies to the study. The researcher comprehensively addressed all the factors and effectively brought them into action. Criterion validity incorporates different specific methods for analyzing the data and obtaining a conclusive result. The researcher thoroughly addressed all the research standards in the study and obtained effective and accurate findings as a result. Construct validity creates a strong relationship between the techniques selected and the instrument used for furnishing the construct of the study (Gioia et al., 2013).

The study did not include personal interpretations of the findings or bias that affected the outcome. According to Leedy and Ormrod (2010), "The researcher should suspend any pre-conceived notions or personal experiences that may unduly influence what the researcher hears the participants saying" (p. 153). Researchers refer to such presupposed ideas as *epoché* or *bracketing*. In the study, the researcher asked sixteen structured questions and eleven open-ended questions to obtain responses concerning the importance and meanings of the lived experiences of how home foreclosures affect physical and mental health. The participants received questions in advance to afford them the chance to clarify their thoughts and perceptions of their lived ordeal.

The researcher analyzed transcribed data from the research and used thematic analysis to decode the data into core themes. An extensive review of the data led to the core themes. The environment where the research took place also ensured external validity. Data generated from the research are only valid and meaningful if they are applicable beyond the research (Leedy & Ormrod, 2010). To solidify the external validity of this research, the study involved interviewing volunteers who went through the foreclosure process instead of conducting research in a laboratory.

The study on distressed homeowners who went through the process of foreclosure supported a phenomenological design. To ensure validity and support the semistructured interview process, the research questions were consistent for each participant (see appendix B). To ensure the accuracy of the data generated, the participants reviewed their responses. The study participants supported the inferences drawn in the current study to understand the potentially negative consequences of home foreclosures on mental and physical health. Leedy and Ormrod (2010) posited the participant validation method involves delivering study findings to participants and requesting feedback that the findings are valid.

Factors including criterion-related validity, construct validity, and content validity indicated the validity of the study. These factors enable the research objectives and research questions to explain the research aims and research questions adequately. These factors also help highlight the ability and capacity of the researcher in extracting the facts about a significant phenomenon or theme (Yin, 2009). The study included validated instruments including mortgage foreclosure study interview questions to address the validity of the data.

The validity of the study also guides the methods used for assessment and analysis, thereby explaining the significance of the study. The study included several methods for ensuring the validity of the research remains high. To reduce the error rate and improve the validity of the research, the researcher minimized false and faulty opinions by not including vague statements. The same approach served to prevent biased results. The participants were motivated to take part in the interviews and answer honestly without any bias and vagueness (Yin,

2009). Vagueness and bias harm the validity of research, as the resulting data are not comprehensive and lack quality.

When participants lack knowledge and information about the theme of the topic and about the core purpose of the research, they feel hesitant to give sincere and honest answers. To maintain the validity of this research, all the participants of the interviews and questionnaire survey knew the purpose of the study and the theme of the questions. The participants also were aware the study would include quoted excerpts of their answers to extract conclusions. This helped the researcher increase the validity of the data collected through the interviews and questionnaire survey and therefore maintain the validity of the research to high standards.

The participants were aware that the results of the interviews and survey would be for academic purposes and would appear in a publication. Participants received and signed an informed consent form. In accordance with the guidelines of informed consent, the willingness of the participant to carry on with the study or to leave it was significant. Any participant had the right to quit the study at any stage of the study. This contributed to the validity of the study. To improve and enhance the results of the primary data, the researcher used cross-examination, which helped improve the results of the study by reducing the error rate. The cross-examination supported the primary data, as well as related literature, and helped raise the levels of the validity of the study.

Data Analysis

Developing thematic and inductive codes for qualitative research were the main process of data analysis. Analysis involved reviewing transcripts and developing a coding scheme built upon the subthemes and themes that appeared in the interviews. The researcher coded each responder's transcript using the scheme and interview excerpts to examine the participants' statements. The coding system ensured the refinement and capture of the range of experiences discussed in the interviews, which represented a listing of the themes collected.

The interview served to address the following research question: What are the possible negative consequences of home foreclosures on physical and mental health? A methodology designed by Colaizzi (1978) subjected all the data to phenomenological analysis. Waite

(2006) described the specific steps under Colaizzi's methodological framework that guided the study and occurred in a process:

1. The researcher transcribed and read the interview responses from participants to obtain a better comprehension of their lived experiences of the foreclosure process.
2. The researcher reviewed transcripts and gathered significant statements relating to participants' lived experiences during the foreclosure process.
3. The researcher formulated the meanings of all significant statements or phrases based on the research participants' narratives.
4. The researcher organized meanings into themes or clusters.
5. The researcher used themes to delineate the participants' foreclosure experiences.
6. The researcher returned the descriptions to each participant to confirm the validity of his or her experience.
7. The researcher added any new relevant data received as a result of the participants' validation to the final description of their lived experience of the foreclosure process.

Following this methodological framework and bracketing ensured a unified view considering objective and subjective realities (Waite, 2006). The procedures revealed any researcher bias, prevented the researcher's assumptions from shaping the data collection, and prevented the researcher from interposing his thoughts and impressions on the analysis. The process led to the discovery of each individual's lived experience through the foreclosure process without the researcher's imposed memories or perceptions. The researcher recorded daily reflections in a journal to reveal any biases or perceptions to consciousness.

The methodology involved reviewing all transcriptions to obtain a sense of the participants and to distill meaning from each phrase, sentence, and description that pertained to the lived phenomenon under investigation. The invariant constituents from the tested statements received thematic labels to reveal the themes of the lived experiences and to validate the recorded transcripts. The researcher constructed textural, structural, and textural or structural descriptions. The researcher collected and interpreted data from the interview questions to create dialogue using an empirical phenomenological approach and the structure of the experiences (Giorgi, 1985). Moustakas (1994) noted the data collected need analyzing for coherence, clustering, the revelation of structure, meaning configuration, and the circumstances of their occurrence.

The population can be represented to establish a composite delineation of the importance and meanings of the experience by the individual textural structural description (Moustakas, 1994).

Ethical Considerations

The sensitivity of the issue regarding the unknown health-related consequences of home foreclosures greatly influenced the development of the methodology of the study. Anonymity was ensured by addressing all ethical issues that arose (see appendix B). To adhere to the anonymity agreement, the researcher replaced participants' names with fictitious names after transcribing the interviews. All the research subjects volunteered to participate (see appendix A), and the researcher assured them the hierarchical research methodology would not exploit them. The researcher had more than ten years of experience as a housing counselor and had successfully applied several foreclosure mitigation strategies to assist distressed homeowners. The presentation of the questions in the questionnaire took place in a caring and supportive manner, and those involved were aware that the researcher would end the interviews at any time and for any reason without any questions asked.

Ethical guidelines are the recommended guidelines for any research. These guidelines incorporate all the processes and operations carried out under the umbrella of a study. The guidelines help ensure the research carried out is ethically sound and strong. These guidelines also help maintain the neutrality of the study, which is a requirement of the standards of research. In every study, the focus is to remove negative elements so no external or internal means can harm the research. The positive results, once obtained, might help improve the community and the people with respect to the theme of the study and leave an impact on society. The results obtained from a study become more dynamic after implementation and thus become more helpful if the researcher addresses ethics comprehensively and accurately (Miller, Leffingwell, Claborn, Meier, Walters, & Neighbors, 2012). It was important to address the ethics of a study as many benefits resulted from the study. The primary aim of any research is to conduct a study and present reliable knowledge on the topic of the research in an effective manner (Yin, 2009). The study involved following international principles of ethics, which were to transcend geographical, cultural, economic, legal, and political aspects of the ethical considerations.

The identity of the participants, including their names, titles, and contact numbers, remained confidential. All participants signed the informed consent form, so the researcher maintained the data collection process adequately and positively. The primary focus of the researcher was to use authentic and up-to-date resources, so that the collected data were the most relevant to use in the study. This ensured the results were the best and the most optimal, as the methods used were optimal. The primary data used in the study contributed to the credibility of the study. Another important factor was maintaining the validity of the study by focusing on the relevance of the topic and by removing vague data and responses.

It is the primary duty of a researcher to ensure all the data sources and data banks are relevant, comprehensive, and up to date. The researcher ensured the discretion of the interviews by using appropriate research methods. The study, which involved gathering qualitative results, included an effective atmosphere for the participants so they could participate freely, which helped raise the levels of credibility and validity to new higher standards, thereby ensuring best outcomes of the study (Miller et al., 2012). The personal information of all the participants remained confidential, thereby maintaining the ethical credibility of the research.

Pilot (Pretest) Study

A pilot test took place before the qualitative phenomenological study began. To solidify the validity of the questions, the interviewer performed the pilot test with five persons who did not participate in the study. The pilot study did not provide all the findings from the research because some themes and responses were redundant. Thus, the findings represented in Chapter 4 summarize the results and are not representative of every interview question and participant response.

The pilot study centered on distressed homeowners who had gone through the foreclosure process in northern New Jersey. Five potential participants received introductory letters and a copy of the informed consent form for their review and signatures; at that time, the participants were able to ask any questions. Face-to-face interviews began after collecting the signed forms and addressing the individuals' concerns. To avoid redundancy, the researcher transcribed major responses of the participants in a sampling format because the answers from the respondents were similar in nature. The sampling format of the responses allowed the participants to provide the most significant answers to the study's questions.

The purpose of the pilot study was to determine the validity and the correct sequencing of the interview questions. A coding system served to differentiate the pilot study participants from the actual research participants after obtaining their signed consent to be involved in the study. Purposeful sampling is common in qualitative research. Creswell (2009) posited that insight into a phenomenon is better when a limited sample size is the goal in a qualitative phenomenological analysis. Zahavi (2003) noted in Husserl's phenomenological studies, researchers must reflect on objects and then thematize and analyze the acts of consciousness, instead of just paying attention to the objects. Such a process will assist in theory generation. Qualitative research was preferable because the researcher participated actively in understanding the problem under scrutiny. Leedy and Ormrod (2010) indicated the qualitative researcher is able to interpret, analyze, and comprehend any social phenomenon. The current study was phenomenological and transcendental because the foreclosure experience (focus) is conscious (Moustakas, 1994).

Summary

Twenty-five participants participated in interviews regarding the concerns and objectives involved in the research design that focused on the methodology, the types of instruments used to collect information, the target population, and the research questions. Chapter 4 contains the findings obtained by analyzing the interviews conducted with the twenty-five homeowners in the process of foreclosure.

C H A P T E R 4

Data Analysis and Results

The purpose of this qualitative phenomenological study was to examine the participants' lived experiences of the possible negative consequences of home foreclosures on physical and mental health in northern New Jersey. Twenty-five homeowners in the process of foreclosure participated in interviews to investigate the health-related concerns brought about by home foreclosure. To gain insight into the lived experiences of these participants in foreclosure, the researcher conducted twenty-four face-to-face interviews and one telephone interview. To guide data collection, the study included a Colaizzi method of analysis of phenomenological data with semistructured, audio tape recorded, and transcribed interviews. Chapter 1 contained an introduction to the study. Chapter 2 contained the review of relevant literature, and the focus of chapter 3 was on the description of the research method. Chapter 4 contains the results of the study.

Chapter 4 includes the specific analysis of twenty-five interviews with homeowners in the process of foreclosure in the Union and Essex

70

Counties of New Jersey. A pilot study with five struggling homeowners tested and validated the interview questions. The pilot study was necessary because it served as a basis for the interview protocol. After the pilot study, the main study commenced with twenty-five struggling homeowners in the process of foreclosure. The researcher then analyzed the data collected for trends and themes of the participants' lived experiences when going through foreclosure, specifically the consequences on their physical and mental health. Chapter 4 includes an explanation of the data analysis method used to unveil the major themes. The focus was answering the principal research question to understand the possible negative consequences of home foreclosures on physical and mental illness. The primary research question for the qualitative phenomenological study was as follows: What are the possible negative consequences of home foreclosures on physical and mental health? This question necessitated the study and the discovered outcomes.

Data Collection Processes

Collecting information for this research occurred in two stages: Stage 1 comprised the pilot study to solidify the protocol of flow during the interview process and validated the interview questions (see Appendix C) and Stage 2 covered the formal data collection for the analysis. For the survey instrument, open-ended questions helped get to the heart of the issues. Adapting the instrument involved adding the open-ended questions to facilitate the need to investigate and understand the possibly negative consequences of home foreclosures on physical and mental health.

To assist in fully exploring the research questions, twenty-five homeowners in the process of foreclosure formed the population and participated in interviews with semistructured questions. The modes of the interviews were in person or by telephone, and both formats were advantageous in directly gathering information.

Pilot Study

The goal of the pilot study was to clarify the study questions and interview protocol with struggling homeowners to affirm the efficacy of the interview questions. To achieve the goal of understanding this crisis, a sample of five homeowners in the process of foreclosure participated in interviews. The phenomenological approach made it possible for the participants to tell their own stories. Recruiting the study participants involved obtaining the list of homeowners in the process of foreclosure from the free public websites http://www.realtytrac.com and http://www.corelogic.com for property and ownership information in the Essex and Union Counties of New Jersey. No changes occurred to the interview questions (see appendix C), but the pilot study uncovered the need to modify protocol as follows: provide participants with a general overview of the study and provide a list of the interview questions to participants during the interview. The pilot study brought invaluable insight into the study. The pilot study took place in accordance with the identified study plan after obtaining Quality Review Methods and Institutional Review Board approvals. The researcher explained the study parameters and intent to the pilot study participants and obtained their signatures on the informed consent (see appendix B). To assist in gauging the time and flow of the interview, each interview lasted twenty-five to thirty minutes.

The pilot study centered on distressed homeowners who had gone through the foreclosure process in northern New Jersey. Five potential participants received introductory letters and a copy of the informed consent form for their review and signatures; at that time, the participants were able to ask any questions. Face-to-face interviews began after collecting the signed forms and addressing the individuals' concerns. To avoid redundancy, the researcher transcribed major responses of the participants in a sampling format because the answers from the respondents were similar in nature. The sampling format of the responses allowed the participants to provide the most significant answers to the study's questions.

The purpose of the pilot study was to determine the validity and the correct sequencing of the interview questions. A coding system served to differentiate the pilot study participants from the actual research participants after obtaining their signed consent to be involved in the study. Three males and two females all over the age of age of 50 years participated in the pilot study. The pilot participants answered twenty-eight open-ended and closed-ended questions, which provided the research data. The participants reflected on their lived experiences through the foreclosure process, which included their revelations, emotions, and processes. The pilot participants provided their demographic data as three African Americans and two Hispanics. Even though the basic objective of the pilot study was to validate the interview protocol as well as the validity and correct sequencing of the interview questions, four themes were revealed including foreclosure process resulting in hospitalization of family, foreclosure and lack of health insurance, foreclosure and negligence of doctor's prescription and displacement and housing instability as a reason for depression. These themes were much evident and fully discussed after interviewing the actual study participants.

Data Collection

Data collection took place over a two-week period from May 9 to May 24, 2014. The researcher transcribed interview data and categorized the data into themes. Thematic data saturation occurred at twenty-five participants obtained by purposive and snowball sampling. The interview process involved establishing the interview space, describing the intent of the research, and signing the informed consent. The study participants answered the interview questions in an orderly and sequential manner (see appendix C). The researcher asked the demographic questions in the beginning of the interview. The participants understood that the researcher was recording their responses on an audio tape and would transcribe them after the interview. For ease of consistency and transition, the interview followed a scripted guide. The participants had an opportunity to express themselves after answering a formal question to provide more information about their lived experiences in the foreclosure process.

Data Analysis

Data analysis involved using the recommended Colaizzi method. Using this method allowed the researcher to eliminate anomalies in the data that were not useful to the themes. The researcher obtained a full description of the experience of the phenomenon by the participants. From the verbatim transcripts, the researcher considered each statement with respect to significance in describing the experience, recorded all relevant statements, listed each non-repetitive, non-overlapping statement, related and clustered the invariant meaning units into themes, synthesized the invariant meaning units and themes into a description of the textures of the experience, reflected on own textural description and constructed a textural-structural description of the meanings and essences of the experience. The textural description that resulted enabled the construction of each research focus and the accurate translation of the interview notes. Grouping the data helped to translate the textural structural descriptions of their lived experiences into meaning and essence for the purpose of further analysis. To relate to the participants' lived experiences, open-ended questions served to elicit responses. The Colaizzi method helped to analyze individual transcripts and create a thematic analysis.

Interview Thematic Analysis

Demographics of the study participants. The researcher explained the study parameters and selection criteria to the volunteer study participants. Tables 1, 2, 3, and 4 contain summaries of the demographics. Table 5 discusses the thematic development of the interviews. Appendix C details the demographic questions. The researcher randomly selected the study participants. The demographic data captured the following information: respondents' marital status, whether respondents had children, respondents' age, and respondents' educational status. The participants provided the demographic data verbally.

After collecting the data, manual analysis proceeded to determine trends, themes, characteristics, and descriptions. The researcher developed themes from the interviews. The themes helped in analyzing words, phrases, expressions of participants, and opinions of the participants.

The study participants answered twenty-eight open-ended and closed-ended questions, which provided the research data. To ensure the qualitative study was phenomenological, the study participants reflected on their lived experiences through the foreclosure process, which included their revelations, emotions, and processes. The semistructured approach ensured the participants shared their experiences without restrictions on their answers. The final question provided the participants the opportunity to reflect on and express anything they wanted to share about their foreclosure experience. The preferred analysis method for the participants' textural descriptions was the Colaizzi method.

Table 1
Gender of Respondents

Gender	N	%
Male	19	76
Female	6	24

Table 2
Age Group of Respondents

Age range	N	%
21–30	3	12
31–40	6	24
41–50	11	44
50 and above	5	20

Table 3
Ethnic and Racial Distribution of Respondents

Ethnicity or race	N	%
African American or Black	7	28
Asian American	3	12
Hispanic or Latino/a	8	32
White or Caucasian	4	16
Other/None	3	12

Table 4
Marital Status of Respondents

Marital status	N	%
Married	23	92
Unmarried	2	8

Table 5
Hospitalization Due to Illness/Diseases Resulting From Foreclosures

Illness/disease	%
Mental disease, e.g., PTSD	20
Physical injury	20
Depression	100
Suicide/suicidal behavior	20
Cardiac disease	8
Stress/anxiety	100
Alcohol abuse	20
Emotional trauma	100

Thematic development of interviews. Four core themes evolved from the interview questions. The participants fully explained their lived experiences of the potential negative consequences of home foreclosures on mental and physical health during the process of their foreclosure. The data were categorized and the correlating themes were derived through the Colaizzi methodology.

Theme 1: Foreclosure and lack of health insurance. The analysis of responses to interview question 21 led to another theme. The question was as follows: How did your family's health insurance or lack of health insurance affect your healthcare during your foreclosure process? The lack of health insurance affects health care received during the foreclosure process. The lack of health insurance or possessing low-quality health insurance policies during the process of foreclosure led to mental or physical illness. Data analysis revealed 80 percent of participants suffered medical issues due to the absence of or low quality of health insurance programs. Fifty-six percent of the participants who went through the foreclosure process lacked health insurance because they were unable to purchase it directly due to financial troubles. Participant V stated that "Like sickness, my husband is a heart patient. He's taking many medications. I also have a right arm problem and not going to work right now. And my daughter is sick. And my mother is also sick, older mother." The participants who experienced foreclosure tended to have lower insurance rates due to their income levels but were still unable to purchase insurance.

The financial problems of the participants' families were the primary reason they were unable to buy insurance. The analysis also noted that the victims of foreclosure were less educated than unaffected homeowners, unemployed, and had a difficult time finding respectable and dignified jobs. The lack of health care insurance during the process of foreclosure affected many respondents. Some reported they developed chronic diseases because they were unable to visit doctors. Viral diseases affected their children when they were going through the home foreclosure process. Due to the foreclosure process, challenging health conditions, and adverse financial conditions, the family environment became unstable. Distress existed among the family members, who subsequently developed stress and depression.

Many of the participants in the study reported that the lack of health insurance affected most of the elderly people in their family because they were unable to pay the insurance programs. They were unable to afford private medical expenses and suffered great losses. The participants reported children underwent hospitalization for diseases that health-care providers could cure in the early stages. Twenty-four percent of the participants reported their children suffered from asthma. Sixty percent of the participants reportedly faced malnutrition issues while going through the process of foreclosure. Prolonged delays in hospitalization occurred among children suffering from any diseases during the process of foreclosure.

Subtheme: Family health and foreclosure process. Question 24 in the survey that developed this subtheme was "How was your family's health affected during the foreclosure process when a member got sick or injured and did not seek healthcare because of the cost involved?" Participant Y responded as "Yeah, I couldn't take them—my parents—to regular visits to their doctor as I was supposed to due to cost issues." As discussed earlier, financial barriers were challenges for families going through the process of foreclosure. Fifty-six percent of the participants reported they faced financial crisis during an accident or injury to themselves or family. Many governmental programs provide insurance for children but some people are unable to be a part of these programs due to a lack of adequate resources for full coverage. Children's insurance for accidents could provide children the necessary medical care in case of injury. However, the victims of the foreclosure reported they could not afford this health insurance program due to financial challenges.

All the research participants with children and seniors in their homes explained that children and elderly members in the family were the greater victims of home foreclosures. Children are more likely to experience negative psychological consequences from home foreclosure, as they have to move from their homes and neighborhood to poor living conditions and sometimes become homeless. Three participants in the current study were unable to contact any health care specialist or psychologist due to the lack of health care programs. They continued that anxiety and disturbing behaviors were also observed behaviors in their children. Foreclosure and financial crises were the reasons the families were unable to seek treatment in the case of emergencies.

One participant explained that his wife had an accident. One participant explained that his son broke his arm while playing. Three participants reported other emergency incidents for which they were unable to receive treatment because of a lack of medical insurance. They must pay in a medical emergency such as these, but could not do so due to financial barriers. Delay in treatment led to permanent disability or long-term issues from the injuries. Elderly members of the families who developed chronic diseases may die early as they may be unable to pay medical charges because of lack of medical insurance or support programs. The spouses of the study participants suffered equally in the foreclosure process because the level of income decreased and debts needed paying.

Theme 2: Foreclosure process resulting in hospitalization of family. The question in the survey that developed theme 2 was "How did the foreclosure process affect you, your spouse, or members in your family in terms of hospitalization or major medical illness?" The perception of participants on the issue of the home foreclosure process was critical, as they were directly involved with its impacts and associated complications.

Participant X stated, "Well, we still going through the foreclosure process, so—and we still have effects. Sometimes I'll get into these bouts of depression and—especially when I get any letter from my bankers—threatening to foreclose the house—and I had one last week. My heart pressure goes up. I've been in the hospital for thinking too much and—yes, it has affect on us emotionally and physically. Physically I end up in the emergency room. When I'm stressed I go into sickle cell crisis and I end up in the emergency room."

The participants noted home foreclosure started with financial insecurity and economic hardship. In most of the cases, after the foreclosure started, it led to major mental and medical illnesses. Participants' primary fears were that home foreclosure would result in auction or seizure by the government, bank, and other authorities.

The research participants affirmed that home foreclosure led to mental instability. The mental instability occurred in different types of mental disorders, even years after the incident. Mental diseases such as posttraumatic stress disorder (PTSD), hemorrhagic strokes, battered person syndrome, and many more were observed among 20 percent of the participants.

The interviews indicated the participants reported fewer physical injuries than mental harm. Only 20 percent reported physical injury to self or any family member. Health care professionals can treat physical injuries in a shorter period of time. Psychological disorders take a long time to treat. Depression was the most common disorder reported in the victims suffering from home foreclosure, with 100 percent of the participants reporting they had experienced depression. The rate of suicide attempts was also observed. One participant reported his mother committed suicide because of her home loans and home foreclosure. He explained his family was in debt and there was no way out. The entire family had to leave their home to foreclosure and became homeless as a result. At least 20 percent of the interview participants reported they developed suicidal behaviors. Mental instabilities including flashbacks, invasive imagery, nightmares, unease, nervousness, sleeplessness, and hypervigilance were the major negative attributes participants reported concerning their spouses.

The participants reported home foreclosure affected the mental and psychological conditions of family members and spouses and led to hospitalization and traumatic conditions. The development of these mental disorders and instabilities affected the development of children who resided with the family. The children experienced the same trauma as their parents. The children reported disturbing social behaviors to their parents in their schools and neighborhood. Many of the participants reported they underwent hospitalization due to stress and depression. Two of the respondents stated that they developed cardiac diseases due to home foreclosures. Rates of hypertension and renal disease were significantly higher among the participants after adjusting for sociodemographic characteristics. In the two years prior to foreclosure, the participants were more likely to visit the emergency department, have an outpatient visit, or have a no-show appointment. All of the participants who went through the process of foreclosure reported that they had multiple visits to emergency rooms due to stress and anxiety of losing their homes.

Twenty percent of the study participants noted they abused alcohol as a result of the home foreclosure process. Anxiety and unsanitary lodging conditions might have a negative impact on well-being. These impacts are difficult to report but have disturbing and long-term consequences.

Anxiety is part of life. However, excessive anxiety and poor adapting tools exacerbate physical and emotional instabilities. It is acceptable to state that most, if not all, individuals involved in foreclosure have nervousness and anxiety. All the interview participants experienced emotional trauma as a result of losing their home. Stretching and pushing worsens unending physical, mental conditions and harms body functions. Although the number of calls to crisis hotlines and demands for specialists have increased, it is difficult to determine the connection to foreclosure. Participant G stated, "It is extremely discouraging to lose one's home. It speaks to misfortune of security, an inclination of disappointment....It is terrifying and overpowering."

Families in foreclosure may be more powerless against medical emergencies than unaffected families. Sickness, with its related expenses and missed employment opportunities, accelerates countless defaults and results in foreclosure filings. For people who are sick, the anxiety of foreclosure may be especially critical. The possibility of moving and relocation due to foreclosure makes it difficult for families to cope with.

Episodes of spousal and child abuse may increase in family units under the anxiety of foreclosure. Money-related anxiety was a significant contributor to household savagery. Although there is no confirmation that a relationship exists between money-related anxiety and foreclosure, some of the participants indicated they and their spouses spoke in raised voices on occasion during their foreclosures due to the internal turmoil during the foreclosure process.

Subtheme: Foreclosure and negligence of doctor's prescriptions. The question number 25 in the survey that developed theme 2 was "How was your family's health affected during the foreclosure process because of neglecting to fill prescription because of the cost involved?" Participant E answered that "Yeah, there were prescriptions that we were supposed to fill but the cost involved, and that is to pick it up and that made the illness worse." Participant H responded, "Oh, so much stress, in the sense that just imagine that you have a baby in your house, and with this foreclosure process, it impacts the entire family in many ways—and gets a whole lot of effects on the whole family....You know and if you look on the bill, you look on your foreclosure issues, you know, it's too much. So what happened is whatever little treatment that she gets, you have to bring her home, because you cannot afford it. You know? You cannot afford to pay that—technically, if not the foreclosure issues, the baby needs to be in the hospital and get any necessary treatment that she deserves, you know, to be better."

Fifty-two percent of the study participants explained they went to the trauma room or to the emergency room during the process of foreclosure but were never able to see any specialist as prescribed. They also explained that their children and spouses suffered many issues, including injuries and accidents. The participants reported that, due to the lack of financial support and lack of money, they were not able to continue their medical health care in the case of injuries, accidents, or chronic diseases.

Participants reported they were not able to follow a doctor's prescription, even if they were able to see a doctor. The prescription might involve some diagnostic tests and medical drugs. The delay in the process of diagnosis prolonged the time of treatment, which led to situations where the study participants were unable to meet the challenge and developed more stress and depression. Three of the participants or their spouse became suicidal. Six study participants reported their families developed viral diseases that worsened because they were unable to follow up and were unable to fill a doctor's prescription. The elderly members of the families who supported themselves died early from a chronic disease because they were unable to obtain medical prescriptions.

Theme 3: Foreclosure as perceived loss of money and ownership. The question 26 in the survey that developed theme 3 was "How did your foreclosure process affect your health as a result of loss or perceived loss of your wealth in your homeownership?" Lack of adequate finances has been a major social issue, such as domestic violence, child abuse, and home foreclosure. Domestic violence—whether physical, psychological, or sexual—does not exist alone. Rather, it occurs with other stressors such as home foreclosure. Participant E stated, "Okay. I think the government should help families with housing foreclosure problems because we save this for—these children are the future of the country, and if we end up in the street, or maybe a shelter, they couldn't afford to go to school. Separation of marriage will come through foreclosure, and that would displace these children, and eventually they will end up in the streets. That will increase the crime rate. If ten families are thrown into the streets due to foreclosure, the results in the future will end up like more crime."

Participant E continued, "And the effects on families could be daunting. There was a time that I was thinking of killing myself—it can cause suicide, and unnecessary criminal behaviors, domestic violence. So no family wants to experience foreclosure. So I think the best thing the government has to do is to help families, especially people with children who are going through foreclosure. The bank is supposed to help the families so that we can help our children."

The consequences of these stressors depend on constituents such as the amount of time elapsed and the amount of wealth lost due to home ownership. Individuals in the United States perceive home foreclosure as a matter of embarrassment and degradation and consequently its effects can manifest themselves in physical aggression, violent actions such as threats, humiliation, and other forms of psychological disturbance that affect children and spouses. This causes emotional disturbances among the participants and leads to many disturbances in their attitudes. This condition is the first step toward the psychological problems of the participant. Their peace of the mind is lost and disturbed.

The foreclosure process affects health as a result of the loss or perceived loss of wealth and homeownership. All the participants suffered depression and stress because of the foreclosure and being as the stressor for the whole family. Foreclosure becomes the reason for the isolation of the participant from social activities and loneliness dominates the patterns of living. If actually foreclosed, the participant must leave their home, neighborhood, and luxuries. Isolation and loneliness result in a situation where the victim tries to find peace of mind and might engage in alcohol or drug abuse, which leads to great disturbances within the family.

The participants shared their concerns about participating in an interview for the current study, as they feel helpless against the plots of crafty relatives and voracious mortgage banks. In two occurrences, corrupt relatives might have put an older adult's housing in danger with a bad refinancing agreement. Older Americans generally depend on their homes for economic security and as a nest egg in retirement. While this may still be the case for many people, as indicated in the participants' demographics, mortgage holders progressively convey contract obligation into their retirement years, with more than half of all family units, with the breadwinner fifty years or older.

Theme 4: Displacement and housing instability as a reason for depression. The question 28 in the survey that developed theme 4 was "We are interested in your story. Feel free to add any comments or explanations for the above questions that may help us understand your situation." Participant C shared her own story:

"What I would do to help people is that when people, if they can't pay their mortgage, there must be process to help quickly. Even with me, I was telling the bank for like a year or two years that I cannot continue to pay this amount of monthly mortgage. So, is there any process because I really don't want to stop payin'—and I was living in my home for eight years. I paid, paid, paid, I was even paying more, I was paying more, I was paying more and my daughter went to college, my brother got sick, died, my sister got sick died, me and myself, everything went up.…The gas went up, the food went up. So if the bank or if somebody say, "Oh, I can't pay but can you reduce it," it's a matter of maybe reducing it, like if I'm staying there for ten years and the mortgage was like thirty years."

The participant continued to explain that the banks should assist homeowners by possibly extending the term of the mortgage and make it more affordable for the struggling homeowner. The participant ended by stating, "I think the bank should be able to do this instead of calling people, calling people, calling people. The bank's behavior causes a lot of stress and depression because they don't listen." There is a general concern that foreclosure is the first step to housing instability for previous homeowners and leaseholders, yet without solid information, there is no acceptable reply to when, where, how, or if families in foreclosure are rehoused. All the study participants in the mortgage foreclosure study saw their credit scores fall, which makes it difficult to buy or rent an alternate home. Eighty percent of the respondents indicated their doctors prescribed a higher dose of their high-blood pressure medication. The thought of housing instability caused about half of the respondents not to be able to eat properly and led to insomnia. Forty percent noted they experienced physical pain thinking about possible displacement and not knowing where their family might end up. Other significant discoveries included marital problems resulting from arguments, lack of sexual desire in the couple, work problems resulting from emotional outbursts because of their inability to control their emotions due to their internal turmoil.

The thought of displacement and possible instability in living arrangements was a source of depression to all the respondents interviewed. They felt overwhelmed by the foreclosure process because of the above consequences, as well as other consequences mentioned by respondents, including facing a highly uncertain future, borrowing money from family and friends, having low energy levels, experiencing heart problems, thinking suicidal thoughts, undergoing credit issues as a result of foreclosure, and poor outcomes for unsuspecting children. Regardless of the possibility that a family can find someone willing to lease to them, many participants indicated they used their funds during the foreclosure process, which made it difficult to provide initial deposits.

Leaseholders may receive short notice of an eviction that results due to the foreclosure of their building. If leaseholders do not leave after receiving a notice of eviction, landlords may sue them, with the ensuing claim remaining on their rental record. The individuals who do leave might not receive rent or security deposit they may use to secure another unit.

The homeless shelters typically report an increase in individuals served, which might indicate that both previous homeowners and tenants are experiencing homelessness. All the research participants indicated they felt these increases would continue to develop, given that a first move for families encountering foreclosure may be to move in with family and friends. As these housing options weaken, more families will become homeless.

Summary

Chapter 4 contained the research findings that identified and explained the negative consequences of the lived experiences on physical and mental health of distressed homeowners who went through the process of home foreclosures. The purpose of the qualitative phenomenological study was to examine and understand the participant's lived experiences of the potential negative consequences of home foreclosure on mental and physical health. The Colaizzi phenomenological analysis method assisted in data collection and analysis to uncover four core themes. The four themes included foreclosure process resulting in hospitalization of family and foreclosure associated with the lack of family's health insurance, family health and the foreclosure process and foreclosure and the negligence of doctor's prescription, foreclosure as perceived loss of money and homeownership and finally displacement and housing instability as a reason for depression.

Chapter 5 contains the conclusions from the study on the negative consequences of home foreclosures on the mental and physical health of distressed New Jersey homeowners in the process of foreclosure. Chapter 5 includes the four core themes that emerged from the analysis and interpretation of the data in chapter 4, as well as the limitations, conclusions, and recommendations for further research.

Conclusions

The purpose of the qualitative phenomenological analysis was to examine the participant's lived experiences of the potentially deleterious consequences of home foreclosures on physical and mental health among people in northern New Jersey, using semistructured and transcribed interviews. The conclusions augmented the body of information on the debilitating physical and mental illness caused by home foreclosures on individuals and families and could help in policy responses to help struggling homeowners.

Discussion

Foreclosure is the legal process that a bank or mortgage company must follow to take ownership of a property after a borrower defaults on a mortgage. In states where the law recommends a judicial approach, the procedure begins when a bank or mortgage company sues the borrower for neglecting to make agreed-upon installment payments. The mortgager and mortgagee must then appear in court, where the bank must prove the case is legitimate. If the judge agrees that the borrower is in default, he or she sets a date when the bank will sell the property. Typically, the borrower does not show up in court, which leads to the passage of a default judgment.

Some states have a nonjudicial foreclosure process. In these states, when lenders discover borrowers to be in default on the home loan, they send a notice of foreclosure or notice of default to the borrowers with a duplicate to the recorder of deeds. The lender sets the date of the prospective sale of the property according to the home loan terms. Should the borrower dispute the validity of the mortgage obligation, he or she must sue the lender to end the foreclosure process. Under either approach, the borrower can avert foreclosure by meeting all past-due commitments or entering into a workout understanding with the mortgage company. When either of these happens, the foreclosure procedure closes by recording a proper notice with the recorder of deeds.

Under both legal frameworks, if the borrower is unable to stop the procedure, the property becomes available for purchase at an auction and title transfers to the highest bidder. Lenders typically set a minimum sale price and if there are no offers over that value, the title returns to the lender. If this happens, the property becomes real estate owned. In most places, if the property is under lease, the occupants face eviction upon exchange of the title, regardless of whether they have been paying their rent. They no longer have the legal protections they had with the previous owner.

Involved in every foreclosure is a family, or numerous families, whose lives will change. Although change is not always negative, the process can involve anticipated worry that the foreclosure process will lead to poor outcomes. Family units usually enter foreclosure when an incident such as divorce, unemployment, sickness, or death in the family significantly changes a family's financial circumstances. Notwithstanding these events, a greater part of the current foreclosure wave occurred because of unsatisfactory or bad credit, a sharp decline in property valuations, and a decline in the overall business climate of the housing market.

The current economic problems aggravated the already bad situation for families attempting to recover from foreclosure. Many families became fiscally helpless and might encounter diseases, unemployment, or other trauma. Although this is not surprising for families facing fore-closure, the number of family units in crisis, coupled with the economic downturn, fueled the issues. Families in foreclosure need help during a period when individuals, organizations, and establishments that may be conventional support systems are overburdened and underfunded. With unemployment climbing, returning from an unemployment situation is significantly more difficult. Despite the fact that foreclosure is difficult for families and even more difficult in the midst of challenging economic circumstances, research on the unknown physical and mental foreclosure-related consequences on families has been lacking.

To fill the gap on foreclosure-related consequences, the current study revealed what has happened to families when they moved for reasons compelled by negative events. Although foreclosure has a few components that separate it from different manifestations of eviction, the study helps to determine the expected consequences of foreclosure on families. The researcher spoke with individuals at danger of and in foreclosure to accumulate their perspectives on what happens to families.

When foreclosures occur, the families living in repossessed properties must usually move. Different impacts might affect almost all aspects of their lives. The current study involved examining foreclosure-related consequences on families and these consequences are grouped into three classes: (a) displacement and housing instability; (b) financial insecurity and economic hardship; and (c) personal and family stress, disrupted relationships, and ill health. These consequences vary for families in different categories. A key component when understanding and foreseeing potential effects is a family's residency status, such as homeowner or leaseholder. As the crisis started to unfold, arrangement concerns centered on homeowners; however, later studies indicated rental units comprise a sizeable number of all repossessed units. Center for Responsible Lending (2007) assessed the rental unit component at 38 percent, yet it is as high as 45 percent for New England and 60 percent in New York City. Children and senior citizens might have specific needs and may be liable to specific foreclosure-related effects.

Although researchers have built an impressive data set recently about a few parts of the foreclosure crisis, including its rate, causes, and suggestions for the fiscal framework, little research exists on its neighborhood effects. One reason is the recency of the crisis. Analysts have not had sufficient data to assemble and analyze what has been occurring, which makes the current study relevant.

One reason for the lack of data about effects of foreclosure on families is that families affected by foreclosure are difficult to find and track. After the bank serves the notice of foreclosure and not long after the completion of the foreclosure, the family living on the property, whether a leaseholder or a homeowner, ordinarily moves out; there is no simple way to find them. Collecting the new addresses for these families, as might be necessary for a dependable study on how they the foreclosure process affected them, is difficult. This was observed when the participants were asked to tell their own story, and 52 percent indicated they did not know where they would be going with their families in the event of eviction.

Despite the fact that little research exists on what happens to families postforeclosure, there has been abundant research on what happens to families after they move for other reasons (Kachura, 2011). Research relating to families compelled to move due to issues in their lives such as unemployment, family changes, and sickness was especially applicable to this issue. Information from nonprofit organizations, housing counselors, and government organizations whose staff manage families in danger of foreclosure was helpful. Although these people cannot report with conviction on what happens to families after foreclosure, they have been close enough to offer sensible theories about likely results. Their perspectives on the attributes of these families and on what may be happening to them offer a premise for possible recommendations.

Losing a home through foreclosure is not a solitary event. In the United States, this is a regularly extended and disturbing process that usually starts with home loan issues and might lead lenders to initiate the foreclosure process, which might lead to eviction and repossession of the home. U.S. banks hold home foreclosure and sale proceeds in their entirety; however, in the United Kingdom and other countries, net benefits after settling obligations for the most part come back to homeowners (Robertson et al., 2008). In the United States, the foreclosure procedure varies considerably by state, might include legal supervision, and can take from a few months to over a year. Therefore, home foreclosure can be an unpleasant life situation of extended duration, with different periods of intensity. Foreclosure is an unpleasant life situation. On the Social Readjustment Rating Scale, which rates the unpleasantness of forty-three life events, foreclosure was initially at number 21 in 1967 (Holmes & Rahe, 1967). If foreclosure-related anxiety surpasses one's capability to cope, it might unduly influence the mental capabilities of the affected individual and his or her well-being and might lead to critical diseases such as cardiovascular diseases.

Potential psychological responses to home foreclosure. The knowledge of distressing life situations exists in the etiology of both tension and depressive issues. Distressing life situations causally relate to the initiation of despondency. The intensity of the foreclosure process might make it particularly malicious. Others problems in a distressing life situation may lead to sadness. Initially, the distressing situation creates the impression that perpetual stressors (e.g., occupational problems, financial constraints) can intensify the effect of unfavorable life events on sadness, especially when they are concordant. Home foreclosure regularly happens in the middle of extensive economic and budgetary troubles, and accordingly might relate to perpetual stressors with unpleasant consequences. Researchers have connected economic stress with depressive symptomatology in populations from the United States, United Kingdom, and China (Krause, 1987; Krause et al., 1998). It appears that the home loan industry misled some borrowers into the misery that may be overlooked by policymakers. Also of particular concern is the inability of homeowners to control the foreclosure proceedings, which might likewise escalate the effect of anxiety on despondency. The current study revealed that the participants felt discouraged and could act to exacerbate unpleasant life situations; for example, their financial issues caused interpersonal clashes both at home and at their workplace. Woodard (2012) noted according to a study published in the creators syndicate, overall physical abuse increased by 0.79 percent per year during the period 2000–2009, while traumatic brain injury increased by 3 percent because of home foreclosures. All these issues can culminate in health problems, and the foreclosure crisis might have aggravated them.

Potential impact of home foreclosure on health behaviors. Some people adopt unhealthful practices to cope with distressing life situations. A connection exists between anxiety and unhealthy practices such as tobacco use, liquor use, dysregulation of rest, and weight gain, but may decrease through physical activity (Finlay-Jones & Brown, 1981). Home foreclosure might also affect health insurance use. The study revealed fiscally challenged homeowners report fewer preventive specialist visits and lower physician-recommended prescription adherence. Finlay-Jones and Brown (1981) asserted that in a bad economy, this might increase, as a recent review indicated that given the economic problems for many Americans forty-five years old and older with established exchanges to nonspecific or non-physician–endorsed pills, 16 percent deferred preventive consideration, and more than 20 percent postponed visiting a doctor.

Significance of Findings

Following are the four core themes developed from the interviews in the process of thematic analysis.

Foreclosure and lack of health insurance. The lack of the health insurance affects health care during foreclosure process. The lack of health insurance or having low-quality insurance policies during the process of foreclosure leads to increased incidence of reported mental or physical illness, as identified in theme 1. Medical issues occur due to the absence of health insurance programs. Financial problems of the families were the primary reason they were unable to buy health insurance policies. Approximately 25 percent of uninsured U.S. residents (approximately 11 million people) participate in a state program (Kaiser Family Foundation, 2013).

People that have experienced foreclosure were more likely to be less educated, be unemployed, and have experienced financial difficulties, making it difficult for them to secure respectable jobs and leading to the occurrence of their home foreclosure. At least half of the participants in the study reported that lack of health insurance affected most of the elderly people in the family because they were unable to pay for insurance. Participants reported children underwent hospitalization for diseases that health care providers could cure at the early stages. The satisfaction of basic needs by these families, as identified by Maslow's needs hierarchy theory, appears affected because of the lack of health insurance.

Family health and foreclosure process. Leaders at the World Health Organization recognize home foreclosures in United States as a public health issue in the absence of health insurance, which negatively affects the physical and emotional sense of the victims, their sense of security, and the consequent increase in spending in this area (Lashley et al., 2009). Each act of foreclosure generates losses in the physical, cognitive, social, moral, and emotional spheres equally among all the participants in the family.

There appear to be health consequences of a homeowner and his or her spouse's health while going through home foreclosure in the United States. Many research participants in this subtheme indicated children and elderly members in the family were the bigger victims. During times of economic uncertainty, the right to health care requires special protection. Individuals with preexisting conditions and other health issues who resided in areas with high versus low foreclosure risk reported a poorer health status (Schootman, Deshpande, Pruitt, & Jeffe, 2012).

Children are more likely to have psychological consequences from experiencing home foreclosure, as they must move from their homes and neighborhood to poorer living conditions and sometimes become homeless. Introversion, passivity, or silent behaviors are common behaviors in preschoolers who experience or witness home foreclosure (Been, Ellen, Schwartz, Stiefel, & Weinstein, 2010). Infants who have experienced home foreclosure have sleeping problems and disturbed living patterns that results in poor weight gain (Lashley et al., 2009). Although one move might be traumatic for a family, multiple moves might lead to poor results for children.

Foreclosure might be a way of activating housing precariousness for families, which could have significant and enduring effects on youngsters. The lack of a stable home can adversely affect conduct and social improvement. Negative consequences exist between changing schools and scholastic achievement. Housing insecurities can also repress guardians' ability to keep a steady bedtime, mealtime, or homework plan, all of which can have negative results for kids. The long-term effects of housing unsteadiness can negatively affect adolescents.

The families reported having more emergency incidents but noted they were unable to receive treatment because they lacked medical insurance. Researchers of a study by public health; emerging public health crisis linked to mortgage default and foreclosure (2011) indicated 32 percent of delinquent homeowners reported much higher levels of medication nonadherence due to cost compared to only 5 percent of nondelinquent participants. The families faced financial difficulties and were not able to pay their health insurance costs. Delays in treatment processes led to permanent disability or long-term issues from the diseases. Participants reported elderly members of the family who developed some chronic diseases died early, as they were unable to pay medical charges because of a lack of medical insurance or support programs.

Foreclosure process resulting in hospitalization of family. The data in theme 2 revealed the participants reported fewer physical injuries to health care professionals. Physical injuries are treatable faster, and psychological disorders take longer to treat. Depression was the most common disorder found in the victims undergoing home foreclosure and its associated psychological disorder. Depression was common because of the mental trauma participants faced. Twenty percent of the participants noted they developed disturbing suicidal behaviors and in some cases attempted suicide. A recent study on suicide revealed the consequences of foreclosures, as suicides had increased to nearly 13 percent among adults forty-six to sixty-four years old during the period 2005 to 2010 (Houle & Light, 2014; *Suicide, US Foreclosures Drive Up Suicide Rate*, 2014). Mental instabilities including flashbacks, invasive imagery, nightmares, unease, nervousness, sleeplessness, hypervigilance, and evasion of distressing triggers were the main negative attributes participants observed in their spouses. The psychological outcomes of the events of home foreclosure are of greater significance to an individual's health because they are lifelong and more harmful for the victims (National Alliance on Mental Illness, 2013).

The interruption, removal, and economic effects of foreclosure are considerable and have debilitating consequences on families. Repercussions may occur in numerous areas, from child rearing to developing respect toward oneself as turmoil, apprehension, and vulnerability accelerates. Extended financial problems and the home foreclosure process encourage conjugal issues and aggravate negative practices including child, spouse, drug abuses, addictions, and so on.

Rates of hypertension and renal disease were likely to be observed among homeowners in the foreclosure process. In the two years prior to foreclosure, these homeowners were more likely to visit the emergency department, have an outpatient visit, and have a no-show appointment. Therefore, there appear to be a strong significance between the foreclosure processes and the hospitalization of participants, children, and spouses. The data suggested that the lack of a family health plan exacerbated the situation.

Foreclosure and negligence of participants to doctor's prescriptions. Fifty-two percent of the participants explained they sought the trauma center or went to the emergency room during the process of foreclosure but were never able to report that they saw any specialist as prescribed. They also explained their children and spouses suffered issues such as injuries and accidents. Due to a lack of financial support, the families were not able to continue their medical health care in the case of injuries, accidents, or chronic diseases.

Participants reported they were not able to follow doctors' prescriptions, even if they saw a doctor. The prescription might involve some diagnostic tests and medical drugs. A delay in the process of diagnosis prolonged the time of treatment for diseases, which led to a condition in which the participants were unable to meet the foreclosure-related consequences and developed more stress and depression as identified in this subtheme.

The mental disorders, mental instabilities, and illnesses caused by home foreclosure require adequate attention of the participants. This requires visits to doctors and psychologists regularly for checkups. Frequent visits to psychologists cause victims not to collaborate with the care providers because they lack confidence and economic resources. Patients' anger increases when someone from the community, family, friends, or children questions them about their visits to a psychologist. Isolation, loneliness, and lack of confidence result in a significant decrease in the parenting capacity of the mothers. The deficiency in the parenting capacity results in a lack of interest in family matters, leading to barriers in the cognitive development and bringing up of children.

Foreclosure as perceived loss of money and ownership. The foreclosure process affects health as a result of the loss or perceived loss of wealth and homeownership. The perceived loss of home and wealth due to foreclosure generates many other social, psychological, and mental issues that lead to the development to diseases such as PTSD and depression.

The monetary challenges connected with foreclosure are onerous. Negative changes to credit scores influence homeowners' ability to move to another house and diminish their capability to get credit for other purchases. Poor credit scores might also adversely affect terms and costs for loans and might prevent them from finding good jobs. The total assets for homeowners in foreclosure decrease, because they lose their home along with any equity and the assessment of favorable circumstances associated with homeownership. The event of a seizure of the property compromises the family's safety and security, as noted in Maslow's needs hierarchy theory (1943).

In the mid-1990s, researchers for the Family Housing Fund in Minneapolis indicated the average family lost $7,200 through foreclosure (Family Housing Fund, 1995). According to theme 3, all the participants indicated they suffered depression and stress because of the foreclosure and its consequences being a stressor for the whole family. Foreclosure becomes the reason for the isolation of the victim from the social activities; acculturation vanishes from the victim and loneliness dominates. These individuals develop mental disorders, mental instabilities, and mental illnesses. The perceived loss of home and wealth generates many other social, psychological, and mental issues that lead to the development of diseases such as PTSD and depression. The mental instabilities lead to the development of PTSD (National Alliance on Mental Illness, 2013). Additionally, the number of families who receive assistance from private sources (individuals, nourishment banks, and so on) or access open aid remains unknown. The states with the highest rates of foreclosure (Nevada, Florida, Arizona, and California) saw their sustenance stamp caseloads increase by nearly 20 percent in 2008 (*The Guardian*, 2013).

Although abundant research is available regarding the fiscal impacts of foreclosure, particularly for older Americans, not a lot of research exists to address the length of time it took to address the potential issues and consequently describe its vitality. Researchers at AARP reported that in the last half of 2007, 28 percent of all contract misconducts and foreclosures were by family unit heads age 50 and older (Fleck, 2011). Fleck noted the foreclosure rate of persons older than 50 is twice the national rate and recommended that persons with unstable earnings learn to manage high-risk levels.

Displacement and housing instability as a reason for depression. According to theme 4, all the participants stated emphatically that they experienced severe stress during the process of foreclosure that causes sleepless nights when they think of possible displacement and relocation. The participants may have experienced self-actualization in Maslow's hierarchy of needs but will be completely shattered in the event of a possible displacement (Maslow, 1943). Such a loss severely affected the growth and development of the participant, who found it difficult to recover.

Occupants of abandoned properties must move frequently. Researchers at the National Coalition for the Homeless (2009) asked, "Why are people homeless?" in a review of homeless coalitions, and they accepted responses from gatherings in twenty-nine states. The most successful action plan was staying with family and friends, and many talked of families going to crisis sanctuaries and actually living in the city, despite the fact that many people thought previous homeowners with more assets could find places to lease.

Tenants might not experience the same sort of monetary effects from foreclosure; they might be affected negatively. As noted above, tenants might not accept monies to which they are entitled. A move might lead to unfavorable housing circumstances, such as an increase in monthly family expenses for rent, utilities, and transportation. Saegert, Fields, and Libman (2011) noted serial displacement is a loss of capital, physical resources, social integration, collective capacity, and psychosocial resources at each of these scales. These losses have negative implications for the health of individuals and groups, within generations as well as across generations.

The fiscal significance of foreclosure is large. However, foreclosure does not result in investment hardship for all families; rather, it is contingent upon their possessions and employment status. Many individuals in the foreclosure process might experience financial hardship. The increase of home loan defaults and foreclosure rates in the 1990s also involved an increase in individual bankruptcy. Some families encountering foreclosure are exhibited in the bankruptcy filing and different measures of investment hardships. Hardship is most straightforward to see in the lives of distinct families that file for bankruptcy as they lose everything, have no place to live, and must begin again.

Beginning again is often not an option for older Americans. The literature does not include research on the effect of foreclosure on older adults; however, given the overwhelmingly antagonistic economic consequences coupled with declining home values, we can expect more

Americans affected by foreclosure will be especially hit hard, given the restricted time frame of foreclosure processing.

As no sound research exists on where families move after foreclosure, it is unclear how the properties and neighborhoods where dispossessed families at one time existed contrast with their new areas. For homeowners, the decrease in budgetary assets and credit standing do not indicate a move toward a positive change. Rentals can be more expensive than owning a home of identical size and quality, which indicates that families will most likely be unable to bear the cost of something better or even to find something equal to their residence preceding foreclosure. Some leaseholders might have a history of housing insecurities that increases with the foreclosure-related move.

Housing insecurity is a challenge for families hit hard by instability and change. Moving, especially eviction, frequently affects older adults negatively. Moving can trigger physical setbacks from which older adults might not recover. It is critical for older adults to find new residences. Goodison (2014) noted a study in the American Heart Association's journal found that each foreclosed property within 328 feet of a study participant's home led to an average increase of 1.71 mm of mercury in systolic blood pressure. As well-being decreases and freedom diminishes, older adults depend on their associations with relocated residents to help them control and foresee their surroundings as moving becomes progressively out of their control.

Implications

Moustakas (1994) posited that phenomenological research is an investigative research method to evaluate and explore everyday experiences with objectivity and naiveté. The purpose of the qualitative phenomenological research study was to explore the lived experiences and examine the possible negative consequences of home foreclosures on physical and mental health in northern New Jersey. To fulfill the objectives of this study, twenty-five homeowners in the process of foreclosure participated in interviews to investigate the as-yet undetected health-related concerns brought about by home foreclosures.

Four themes emerged during data collection. The four themes were revealed to have significance with the study findings. The four themes were foreclosure linked with the lack of family's health insurance as well as family health and the foreclosure process, foreclosure process resulting in hospitalization of family and foreclosure and the negligence of doctor's prescription, foreclosure as perceived loss of money, and finally homeownership and displacement and housing instability as a reason for depression. This chapter contains highlights of participant comments and supporting literature. The implications are concepts from the study and implications to leadership. The core themes highlighted notable implications of the possible negative consequences of home foreclosures on mental and physical health.

Policy Implications

Two general classes of home foreclosure remediation approaches have gained the most consideration: (a) those who keep the foreclosure procedure in check from the onset and (b) those who defer home foreclosure resulting from home loan misconduct. In the United States, for example, a lot of legislation exists to help homeowners avoid foreclosures by expanding home loan industry oversight, enhancing advance term exposures, and obliging banks to correspond with borrowers before foreclosure begins. The Obama administration has presented the Homeowner Affordability and Stability Plan, which takes into consideration less demanding home loan refinancing options for nonreprobate homeowners, which is different from a strategy proposed by the previous Bush Administration (and embraced by Obama as a competitor) that might have organized national foreclosure moratoria, permitting greater opportunity for renegotiating advance terms preceding expulsion (U.S. Department of Housing and Urban Development, 2013).

Foreclosure prevention strategies have been in the forefront of the national discussions;

it appears that little has been mentioned about their impacts on homeowners and their families. The Homeowner Affordability and Stability Plan strategies employed by the Obama administration officials might help to prevent foreclosures from happening and may be most appropriate to secure the well-being of homeowners at greatest risk of foreclosure. Despite the fact that overextended homeowners' perpetual budgetary strain would likely continue, early intervention approaches might guarantee that people are secure from the impacts of foreclosure-related anxiety, which is different from approaches that broaden or extend the time of foreclosure process before eventual eviction. Such approaches increase the stress of the homeowners in the process of their inevitable eviction under such arrangements.

It is interesting to determine which approaches are most beneficial to reprobate homeowners facing impending eviction in foreclosure. Such strategies might differ significantly across countries given the different opinions in the introduction and delivery of help for what some see as a moral obligation. In the United States for example, it appears to be improbable that foreclosure prevention actions will include the objective of balancing foreclosure and the prevention of physical and mental health because of the rules of the mortgage industry, yet different countries offer valuable models. The United Kingdom made a plan to encourage referrals for mental health screening to assist those facing unemployment and debt obligations, including scores influenced by housing repossession (Bennett et al., 2009). Methods that might help families learn how to budget and live within their means by choosing their housing needs carefully might help prevent rampant foreclosures.

Fast-tracking foreclosures may be beneficial to neighborhoods and the whole community to reduce the overall cost of foreclosures and improve economic recovery. The authors of a recent article published by Ohio.com indicated the amount of time it takes to complete the foreclosure process over six months in Ohio added significantly to the overall cost of foreclosure and slows economic recovery (Effinger, 2014). Reducing the time it takes to complete home foreclosures will reduce blight, crime, and other health consequences to the neighborhood and the whole community.

Many Americans who do not have private insurance have coverage in government programs such as Medicare and Medicaid, as well as other state and local government programs for the poor. One of the goals of the government is to expand the scope of these programs to all segments of the population that need them. Similarly, there is a need to focus on the health care programs of the people who go through the process of home foreclosure. A need exists to develop such policies that will support the health care plan of families going through home foreclosure.

There appears to be a need for compulsory and voluntary medical insurance for children from birth and necessary in the event of any health problems. The most critical social institution that services the victims of any health issues is the hospital. People who go to the emergency room need an insurance plan. In its absence, they must pay for the care received, and their financial status does not allow them to do so.

The right to health care requires special attention and protection. Politicians have to take action not only to manage the care of the sick. They must also take into account the prevention triggered by stressful events such as home foreclosures. There appear to be real dangers of foreclosures to homeowners, and politicians should make relevant decisions to comply with their obligation to hear the parties involved and seek advice from experts.

Limitations

Limitations existed in generalizability and population representation. Data were from twenty-five participants' responses to a semistructured interview questionnaire. Time constraints limited the study. A study is only valid if the research instrument is reliable and valid. A pilot study helped validate interview questions for consistency. Interview questions remained consistent to increase validity.

The researcher applied geographic limitations so the data were all from a specified region, which was New Jersey. Results can vary from one region to the other. According to Creswell (2009), interviewing in the participant's location is a limiting factor. Participant interviews took place at a location without distractions, thereby reducing the limitation of participant location. A research protocol (see appendix B) and the interview questions (see appendix C) guided the participants to help suspend preconceptions, anxieties, and uncertainties. The researcher collected the data from the specific resources, which ensured the authenticity of the collected information. As the basis of the research was the process of foreclosure, the researcher ensured the research involved the data from the victims of foreclosure in New Jersey. Another limitation was the research method selected. The researcher ensured the research involved interviews as the only approach in the qualitative phenomenological approach. Another limitation is the short-term nature of the study where the long-term impact of foreclosure is unknown.

Recommendation for Future Research

The current study revealed the unknown deleterious consequencess of home foreclosures on the mental and physical health of citizens in New Jersey. The findings included several recommendations to manage the social menace of poor health outcomes for families during the foreclosure process. Future research might include a focus on the economic and health consequences of a mortgage company's actions on struggling homeowners when an automatic moratorium occurs with an indication of imminent default. Other future research might include a focus on the possible negative consequences of commercial foreclosures on mental and physical health.

Recommendations to Leaders and Practitioners

Although research on the scope of this predicament was minimal, it is apparent that foreclosures can have negative health consequences on families. Consequences on neighborhoods can also be devastating. Due to the high intensity of foreclosures since 2009, how prepared are Americans to address the health-related effects of home foreclosures?

Two inquiries appear to exist in this problem. As noted, much of the critical measures that must be done to address the crisis eventually must take place at the neighborhood level or within metropolitan regions. A need exists to coordinate and cooperate with city and metropolitan officers and professionals to press for crucial changes in state and elected officials' strategies that will empower a suitable neighborhood response.

A workable neighborhood foreclosure reaction framework should create proper instruments and serve to integrate nearby organizations to (a) develop a coordinated foreclosure response strategy, (b) prevent foreclosures and keep families in their homes, (c) stabilize neighborhoods, and (d) help families recover. Federal and state foreclosure task forces could develop and coordinate sound and workable local foreclosure response systems as strategies to prevent foreclosures from removing families from their homes, to stabilize neighborhoods, and to help affected individuals recover.

A need exists to respect city and metropolitan pioneers and professionals as the essential group of professionals in oversight roles, in spite of the fact that nearby stakeholders need to press for crucial changes in state and elected strategies that will empower a suitable neighborhood reaction. Those involved in helping foreclosed families recover must give consideration to homeowners who might still be financially capable of maintaining an alternate residence, as well as to displaced renters. Emergency housing assistance, financial, or other types might be necessary to help the most troubled and vulnerable homeowners (e.g., those undergoing illness, family stress, or job loss) and renters. They might need housing assistance and in-kind assistance such as food and clothing. In the case of medical emergency, there is a need of any insurance plan for the victims. In its absence they have to pay and their poor financial status do not allow them to do so.

The affected homeowners might benefit from advice on how to restore their credit by helping them learn better financial management skills, how to create a budget, and how to stick with realistic plans in repairing their credit histories (Kingsley et al., 2009). According to Hamlett (2014), the most important first step for any delinquent or foreclosed homeowner getting back on track and regaining financial health is making the decision to seek help. A need exists to focus on the health care programs of people who go through the process of home foreclosure. A need also exists to develop policies that will support the health care plan of the families going through home foreclosure. Cannuscio, Alley, Pagán, Soldo, Krasny, Shardell, and Lipman (2012) noted high foreclosure rates might have broad implications for nursing and public health. The high-risk group of delinquent homeowners might benefit from coordinated, affordable health and social services. Federal and state government officials must help to provide support programs in cases involving older adults and children affected by home foreclosure, especially if an older adult has a chronic disease and are unable to afford medical prescriptions. Politicians have to take action not only to properly manage the care of the sick. Early intervention will prevent early death from preventive support programs.

Conclusions

The focus of data analysis was on identifying core themes in the study. Moustakas (1994) posited the main goal of a phenomenological inquiry is developing meanings from the data to capture the essence of a phenomenon. To ensure the study captured the insights investigated, open-ended interview questions afforded the opportunity for the volunteers to reflect on their lived experiences of the foreclosure process. The twenty-five New Jersey citizens who went through the home foreclosure process reflected on their possible negative experiences on their mental and physical health. Four basic themes emerged, and the finding of the study explained all the themes have strong significance. The significance and the importance of addressing this social issue might help the individuals to meet their health issues even in poor financial conditions while losing their homes to foreclosure.

Summary

The qualitative phenomenological study involved investigating the lived experiences of the consequences of home foreclosures on the physical and mental illness of northern New Jersey homeowners. The study included sampling twenty-five homeowners in the process of foreclosure, investigated the unknown health-related concerns, analyzed the findings, and provided recommendations. The findings of the study will be particularly useful for local practitioners and decision makers in providing a workable local foreclosure response system. Four themes were revealed from the study. The four themes included foreclosure process resulting in hospitalization of family and foreclosure associated with the lack of family's health insurance, family health and the foreclosure process and foreclosure and the negligence of doctor's prescription, foreclosure as perceived loss of money and homeownership, and finally, displacement and housing instability as a reason for depression. The current phenomenological research study of the lived experiences of home foreclosures added to the body of knowledge because it highlighted the stressors, reasons, and causes and provided a framework for identifying the consequences on the physical and mental health of the participants and their families.

References

Ackerman, T. (2010, March/April). Foreclosure vs. homeless: Take a proactive approach. Retrieved from http://www.nala.org/Upload/file/PDF-Files/FactsFindings /Ackerman.pdf

Addy, S., Engelhardt, W., & Skinner, C. (2013, January). Basic facts about low-income children: Children under 18 years, 2011. Retrieved from http://www.nccp.org/publications/pub_1074.html

Alexander, K. L., Entwisle, D. R., & Dauber, S. L. (1996). Children in motion: School transfers and elementary school performance. *Journal of Educational Research, 90,* 3–12. doi:10.1080/0022067 1.1996.994443

Apgar, W. (2008). The mortgage market meltdown and older Americans [Abstract]. Retrieved from http://www.foreclosure-response.org/abstracts.html

Armatrading, J. (1999, September 7). Job insecurity, intensification of work damage British workers' health. Retrieved from http://www.wsws.org/en/articles/1999 /09/uk-s07.html

Armour, M., Rivaux, S., & Bell, H. (2009, March). Using context to build rigor: Application in two hermeneutic phenomenological studies. *Qualitative Social Work, 8,* 101–122. doi:10.1177/1473325008100424

Armour, S. (2008, May 14). Foreclosures take an emotional toll on many homeowners. *USA Today.* Retrieved from http://www.usatoday.com

Balls, P. (2009). Phenomenology in nursing research: Methodology, interviewing, and transcribing. *Nursing Times, 105*(32–33), 30–33. Retrieved from http://www.nursingtimes.net

Been, V., Ellen, V., Schwartz, A., Stiefel, L., & Weinstein, M. (2010). *Kids and foreclosures: New York City.* New York: Furman Center for Real Estate & Urban Policy, New York University. Retrieved from http://furmancenter.org/files /Foreclosures_and_Kids_Policy_Brief_Sept_2010.pdf

Belkic, K. L., Landsbergis, P. A., Schnall, P. L., & Baker, D. (2004). Is job strain a major source of cardiovascular disease risk? *Scandinavian Journal of Work, Environment & Health 30*(2), 85–128. Retrieved from http://workhealth.org /references/review percent20article percent20SJWEH percent20April percent202004.pdf

Benassi, V. A., Sweeney, P. D., & Dufour, C. L. (1988). Is there a relation between locus of control orientation and depression? *Journal of Abnormal Psychology 97,* 357–367. doi: 10.1037/0021-843X.97.3.357

Bennett, G. G., Scharoun-Lee, M., & Tucker-Seeley, R., (2009, June). Will the public's health fall victim to the home foreclosure epidemic? *PLoS Medicine 6*(6): e1000087. doi:10.1371/journal.pmed.1000087.

Bleich, A., Gelkopf, M., & Solomon, Z. (2003). Exposure to terrorism, stress-related mental health symptoms, and coping behaviors among a nationally representative sample in Israel. *Journal of the American Medical Association, 290,* 612–620. Retrieved from http://www.impact.arq.org/doc/kennisbank/1000011125-1.pdf

Bocian, D. G., Li, W., & Ernst, K. S. (2010). Foreclosures by race and ethnicity: The demographics of a crisis. *Center for Responsible*

Lending. Retrieved fromhttp://www.responsiblelending.org/ mortgage-lending/research analysis/foreclosures-by-race-and-ethnicity.html

Bosma, H., Peter, R., Siegrist, J., & Marmot, M. (1998). Two alternative job stress models and the risk of coronary heart disease. *American Journal of Public Health, 88*(1), 68–74. Retrieved from http://www.ncbi.nlm.nih.gov/pmc/articles/PMC1508386/

Brown, G. W., & Harris, T. (1978). *Social origins of depression.* London, England: Tavistock.

Butler, K. (2008, November). Schools feel pain of financial meltdown. *District Administration, 44*(12), 18–19. Retrieved from http:// connection.ebscohost.com/c/articles/35239590/schools-feel-pain-financial-meltdown

Cahill, J. (1983). Structural characteristics of the macroeconomy and mental health: Implications for primary prevention research. *American Journal of Community Psychology 11*, 553–571. doi:10.1007/BF00896805

Calvó-Armengol, A., Patacchini, E., & Zenou, Y. (2009). Peer effects and social networks in education. *Review of Economics Studies, 76*, 1239–1267. doi:10.1111/j.0042-7092.2007.00700.x

Caner, A., & Wolff, E. N. (2004). *Asset poverty in the United States: Its persistence in an expansionary economy* [Public policy brief no. 76]. Annandale-on-Hudson, NY: Levy Economics Institute of Bard College. Retrieved from http://www.econstor.eu/bitstream/10419/54341/1/515646784.pdf

Cannuscio, C. C., Alley, D. E., Pagán, J. A., Soldo, B., Krasny, S., Shardell, M., Asch, D. A., & Lipman, T. H. (2012). Housing strain, mortgage foreclosure, and health. *Nursing Outlook, 60*(3), 134–142. doi:10.1016/j.outlook.2011.08.004

Carey, M. P., & Durant, L. E. (2000). Self-administered questionnaires versus face-to-face interviews in assessing sexual behavior in young women. *Archives of Sexual Behavior, 29*, 309. doi:10.1023/A:1001930202526

Center for Mental Health Services. (2003). *Blueprint for change: Ending chronic homelessness for persons with serious mental illnesses and/or co-occurring substance use disorders* (Substance Abuse and Mental Health Services Administration Pub. No. SMA-04-

3870). Retrieved from http://store.samhsa.gov/pages/searchResult/ percent23SMA-04-3870

Center for Responsible Lending. (2007, March 27). *Subprime lending: A net drain on homeownership* [CRL issue paper 14]. Retrieved from http://www.responsiblelending.org/mortgage-lending/research-analysis/Net-Drain-in-Home-Ownership.pdf

Chapple, A. (1999). The use of telephone interviewing for qualitative research. *Nurse Researcher, 6*(3), 85–93. Retrieved from http://nurseresearcher.rcnpublishing.co.uk/archive/article-the-use-of-telephone- interviewing-for-qualitative-research

Childs, D. (2008). Foreclosure-related suicide: Sign of the times? Retrieved from http://abcnews.go.com/Health/DepressionNews/story?id=5444573&page=1#.UZl wUrU3t6k

Cobaugh, D. J., Angner, E., Kiefe, C. I., Ray, M. N., Lacivita, C. L., Weissman, N.W., & Allison, J. J. (2008, November). Effect of racial differences in ability to afford prescription medications. *American Journal of Health-System Pharmacy, 65,* 2137–2143. doi:10.2146/ajhp080062

Colaizzi, P. F. (1978). Psychological research as a phenomenologist views it. In R. S. Valle & M. King (Eds.), *Existential phenomenological alternatives for psychology* (pp. 48–71). New York, NY: Oxford University Press.

Colledge, M. (1982). Towards a sociological understanding of the impact of the recession on health and illness. *Social Science and Medicine, 16,* 1927. doi:10.1016/0277-9536(82)90391-4

Communities at risk: How the foreclosure crisis is damaging urban areas and what is being done about it. (2009). Retrieved from http://backend.livingcities.org   /_backend.livingcities.org/files/Living_Cities-communities-at-risk.pdf

Connelly, L. (2010). What is phenomenology? *MEDSURG Nursing, 19,* 127–128 Retrieved from http://web.ebscohost.com/ehost/pdfviewer/pdfviewer?sid=7aa9c50e-48e1-4a75-a748-65b44d-68be5b percent40sessionmgr15&vid=2&hid=27

CoreLogic. (2013, May). National foreclosure report. Retrieved from http://www.corelogic.com/research/foreclosure-report/national-foreclosure-report-may-2013.pdf

Creswell, J. W. (2009). *Research design: Qualitative, quantitative and mixed methods approaches.* Thousand Oaks, CA: Sage.

Danermark, B. D., & Ekström, M. (1990). Relocation and health effects on the elderly: A commented research review. *Journal of Sociology and Social Welfare 17*, 25–49. Retrieved from http://connection.ebscohost.com/c/articles/15169603/relocation-health-effects- elderly-commented-research-review

Dooley, D., Fielding, J., & Levi, L. (1996, May). Health and unemployment. *Annual Review of Public Health, 17*, 449–465. doi:10.1146/annurev.pu.17.050196.002313

Duchon, L., Schoen, C., Doty, M., Davis, K., Strumpf, E., & Bruegman, S. (2001). Security matters: How instability in health insurance puts U.S. workers at risk. Retrieved from http://www.commonwealthfund.org/~/media/files   /publications/fund-report/2001/dec/security-matters--how-instability-in-health-insurance-puts-u-s--workers-at-risk/duchon_securitymatters_512-pdf.pdf

Educating the homeless. (2008). *State Legislatures, 34*(5). Retrieved from http://www.questia.com/library/1G1-178454317/educating-the-homeless

Effinger, L. (2014). Foreclosure fast- tracking gains momentum. *National Mortgage News, 38*(34), 16. Retrieved from http://search.proquest.com/docview/1525822434?accountid=458

Eggum, J., Porter, K., & Twomey, T. (2008). Saving homes in bankruptcy: Housing affordability and loan modification. *Utah Law Review, 2008*, 1123–1168. Retrieved from http://ssrn.com/abstract=1349151

Families USA. (2009). Too great a burden: Americans face rising health care costs. Retrieved from http://www.familiesusa.org/resources/publications/reports/too-great-a-burden-2009.html

Family Housing Fund. (1995). Cost effectiveness of mortgage foreclosure prevention. Retrieved from http://www.fhfund.org/_dnld/reports/MFP_1995.pdf

Faravelli, C., & Pallanti, S. (1989, May 1). Recent life events and panic disorder. *American Journal of Psychiatry, 146*, 622–626. Retrieved from http://ajp.psychiatryonline.org/article.aspx?articleid=165930

Fellowes, M. (2006). Credit scores, reports, and getting ahead in America. *Metropolitan Policy Program, The Brookings Institution.* Retrieved from http://www.brookings.edu/research/reports/2006/05/childrenfamilies-fellowes

Finlay-Jones, R., & Brown, G. W. (1981). Types of stressful life event and the onset of anxiety and depressive disorders. *Psychological Medicine, 11,* 803–815. doi:10.1017/S0033291700041301

Fireside, D. (2009). Renters in the crosshairs: Community organizers are fighting for renters facing eviction because of foreclosure. Retrieved from http://www.dollarsandsense.org/archives/2009/0309fireside.html

Fischer, C. T. (2009). Bracketing in qualitative research: Conceptual and practical matters. *Psychotherapy Research, 1*(4-5). doi: 10.1080/10503300902798375

Fischer, K. E., Kittleson, M., Ogletree, R. Welshimer, K., Woehike, P., & Benshoff, J. (2000). The relationship of parental alcoholism and family dysfunction to stress among college students. *Journal of American College Heath, 48*(4), 151–156. Retrieved from http://search.proquest.com/docview/213013318?accountid=45

Fleck, C. (2011). Delinquent homeowners: Many Americans have stopped paying their mortgages and remain in their homes. Retrieved from http://www.aarp.org/money /credit-loans-debt/info-09-2011/foreclosed-and-paying-no-mortgage.html

Furman Center for Real Estate and Urban Policy. (2010). Foreclosed properties in NYC: A look at the last 15 years. Retrieved from http://furmancenter.org/files   /publications/Furman_Center_Fact_Sheet_on_REO_Properties.pdf

Gallo, W. T., Bradley, E. H., Siegel, M., & Kasl, S. V. (2000). Health effects of involuntary job loss among older workers: Findings from the health and retirement survey. *Journals of Gerontology, Series B, Psychological Sciences and Social Sciences 55*(3): S131-S140. doi:10.1093/geronb/55.3.S131

Galuszka, P. (2008). Drastic measures for difficult times. *Diverse: Issues in Higher Education, 25*(22), 16-18. Retrieved from http://diverseeducation.com/

Garson, G. D. (2002). Case study research in public administration and public policy: Standards and strategies. *Journal of Public Affairs Education, 8,* 209–216. Retrieved from http://www.jstor.org/discover/10.2307/40215571?uid=3739672   &uid=2129&uid=2&uid=70&uid=4&uid=3739256&sid=21102289301127

Gerson, K., & Horowitz, R. (2002). Observation and interviewing: Options and choices in qualitative research. In T. May (Ed.),

Qualitative research in action (pp. 17–52). Thousand Oaks, CA: Sage.

Gioia, D.A, Kevin G., Corley, K.G., & Hamilton, A. L. (2013). Seeking Qualitative Rigor in Inductive Research: Notes on the Gioia Methodology. *Organizational Research Methods*. doi: 10.1177/1094428112452151.

Giorgi, A. (1970). *Psychology as a human science: A phenomenologically based approach.* New York, NY: Harper & Row.

Giorgi, A. (1985). Sketch of a psychological phenomenological method. In A. Giorgi (Ed.), *Phenomenological and psychological research* (pp. 8–22). Pittsburgh, PA: Duquesne University Press.

Giorgi, A. (1997). The theory, practice, and evaluation of the phenomenological method as a qualitative research procedure. *Journal of Phenomenological Psychology, 28,* 235–260. doi:10.1163/156916297X00103

Goodison, D. (2014, May 14). Blood pressure spike seen in foreclosure neighbors. *McClatchy-Tribune Business News.* Retrieved from http://search.proquest.com/docview/1524041902?accountid=458

Goux, D., & Maurin, E. (2005). The effect of overcrowded housing on children's performance at school. *Journal of Public Economics, 89,* 797–819. Retrieved from http://www.jourdan.ens.fr/~emaurin/wdocuments/publications/Journal-public-Economics-05.pdf

Gray, M. J., Maguen, S., & Litz, B. T. (2004). Acute psychological impact of disaster and large-scale trauma: Limitations of traditional interventions and future practice recommendations. *Prehospital and Disaster Medicine, 19,* 64–72. doi:10.1017/S1049023X00001497

Green, H. (2008, December). Unretired: Retirees are back, looking for work. *Bloomberg Businessweek Magazine.* Retrieved from http://www.businessweek.com/

Grossi, G., Perski, A., Lundberg, U., & Soares, J. (2001). Associations between financial strain and the diurnal salivary cortisol secretion of long-term unemployed individuals. *Integrative Physiological and Behavioral Science, 36,* 205-219. doi:10.1007/BF02734094

Gruman, D. H., Harachi, T. W., Abbott, R. D., Catalano, R. F., & Fleming, C. B. (2008). Longitudinal effects of student mobility on three dimensions of elementary school engagement.

Child Development, 79(6), 1833-1852. doi:10.1111/j.1467 8624.2008.01229.x

The Guardian. (2013).Which US states have the most people on food stamps? Retrieved from http://www.theguardian.com/world/datablog/2009/may/01/us-states-food-stamps

Gwynne, S. C. (1992). The long haul. *Time Magazine, 140*(13), 34–38. Retrieved from http://www.time.com/

Hamlett, R. (2014, May). Counseling, literacy services needed to prevent foreclosures. *Afro-American.* Retrieved from http://search.proquest.com/docview/1528951258?accountid=458

Hammen, C. (2006, June 29). Stress generation in depression: Reflections on origins, research, and future directions. *Journal of Clinical Psychology, 62,* 1065–1082. doi:10.1002/jclp.20293

Hanushek, E. A., Kain, J. F., & Rivkin, S. G. (2004, August). Disruption versus Tiebout improvement: The costs and benefits of switching schools. *Journal of Public Economics, 88,* 1721–1746. Retrieved from https://www.utd.edu/research/tsp-erc/pdf/jrnl_hanushek_2003_disruption_versus_tiebout.pdf.pdf

Hartley, D. (2010). The impact of foreclosures on the housing market. *Economic Commentary (Cleveland), 2010*(15), 1. Retrieved from http://www.clevelandfed.org/

Healy, J. (2008, November 21). Unable to sell homes, elderly forgo move to assisted living. *New York Times.* Retrieved from http://www.nytimes.com/

Holmes, T. H., & Rahe, R. H. (1967). The social readjustment rating scale. *Journal of Psychosomatic Research, 11,* 213. doi:10.1016/0022-3999(67)90010-4

Houle, J. N., & Light, M. T. (2014). The home foreclosure crisis and rising suicide rates, 2005 to 2010. *American Journal of Public Health, 104,* 1073–1079. Retrieved from http://search.proquest.com/docview/1538587467?accountid=458

Housing program of Jefferson Parish. (2007, June). National foreclosure prevention awareness campaign. Retrieved from http://www.jeffparishsection8.org/index.php /2007/06/25/homeownership/national-foreclosure-prevention-awareness-campaign/

Immergluck, D. (2007, April). Will "streamlining" the mortgage foreclosure process reduce   vacancy and abandonment (Working

Paper WP07DI1). Retrieved from https://www.lincolninst.edu/pubs/dl/1233_Immergluck%20Final.pdf

Institute for Children, Poverty, and Homelessness. (2013). *Foreclosures and homelessness: Understanding the connection* [Policy brief]. Retrieved from http://www.icphusa.org/Publications/American Almanac/

Investopedia.com. (n.d.). Loan modification. Retrieved from http://www.investopedia.com/terms/l/loan_modification.asp

Irvine, A. (2011). Duration, dominance and depth in telephone and face-to-face interviews: A comparative exploration. *International Journal of Qualitative Methods, 10*, 202–220. Retrieved from http://web.wilkes.edu/jennifer.edmonds /MBA_512/Telephone% 20and%20Face to-Face%20Interviews.pdf

Jaromahum, J., & Fowler, S. (2010). Lived experience of eating after esophagectomy: A phenomenological study. *MEDSURG Nursing, 19*(2), 96–100. Retrieved from http://web.ebscohost.com/ehost/detail?sid=265a9620-9f1b-4439-9fe4a-22a173f6a9c% 40session mgr112&vid=1&hid=126&bdata=JnNpdGU9ZWhv c3Qt bGl2ZQ% 3d%3d#db=aph&AN=49783271

Jayasundera, T., Silver, J., Anacker, K., & Mantcheva, D. (2010). Foreclosure in the nation's capital: How unfair and reckless lending undermines homeownership. Retrieved from http://www.ncrc.org/images/stories/pdf/research/ncrc_foreclosure _paper_final.pdf

Joint Center for Housing Studies of Harvard University. (2008). The state of the nation's housing 2008. Retrieved from http://www.jchs.harvard.edu/research/publications/state-nations-housing-2008

Kachura, M. (2011). Children and foreclosures: Baltimore City. An examination of students affected by foreclosures, 2003-2008. Retrieved from http://www.bniajfi.org/uploaded_files/children_ and_foreclosures_report_phase_1_final.pdf

Kaiser Family Foundation. (2013). Key facts about the uninsured population. Retrieved from http://kff.org/uninsured/fact-sheet/key-facts-about-the-uninsured-population/

Kalita, S. (2011, August 1). Tying health problems to rise in home foreclosures. *Wall Street Journal.* Retrieved from http://online.wsj.com/

Kasl, S. V. (1982). Strategies of research on economic instability and health. *Psychological Medicine, 12,* 637–649. doi:10.1017/S0033291700055744

Keith, V. M. (1993). Gender, financial strain, and psychological distress among older adults. *Research on Aging, 15,* 123–147. doi:10.1177/0164027593152001

Kendler, K. S., Gardner, C. O., & Prescott, C. A. (2003). Personality and the experience of environmental adversity. *Psychological Medicine, 33,* 1193–1202. doi:10.1017/S0033291703008298

Kendler, K. S., Karkowski, L. M., & Prescott, C.A. (1998, November). Stressful life events and major depression: Risk period, long-term contextual threat, and diagnostic specificity. *Journal of Nervous and Mental Disease, 186*(11), 661–669. doi:10.1097/00005053-199811000-00001

Kingsley, G. T., Smith, R., & Price, D. (2009, May). The impacts of foreclosures on families and communities. Retrieved from http://www.urban.org/UploadedPDF/411909_impact_of_forclosures.pdf

Korkeila, M., Kaprio, J., Rissanen, A., Koshenvuo, M., & Sörensen, T. I. (1998). Predictors of major weight gain in adult Finns: Stress, life satisfaction and personality traits. *International Journal of Obesity and Related Metabolic Disorders, 22,* 949–957. Retrieved from http://web.ebscohost.com/ehost/pdfviewer/pdfviewer?sid=deb04613-5e994e4a-82cf-e289600b3dea%40sessionmgr10&vid=2&hid=27

Krause, N. (1987). Chronic financial strain, social support, and depressive symptoms among older adults. *Psychology and Aging, 2,* 185–192. doi:10.1037/0882-7974.2.2.185

Krause, N., Liang, J., & Gu, S. (1998, March). Financial strain, received support, anticipated support, and depressive symptoms in the People's Republic of China. *Psychology and Aging, 13,* 58–68. doi:10.1037/0882-7974.13.1.58

Kuipers, B. (1994). *Qualitative reasoning: Modeling and simulation with incomplete knowledge.* Cambridge, MA: Massachusetts Institute of Technology.

Larsen, J. H., Wilson, S. M., & Beley, R. (1994). The impact of job insecurity on marital and family relationships. *Family Relations, 43,* 138–143. doi:10.2307/585315

Lash, A. A., & Kirkpatrick, S. L. (1994). Interrupted lessons: Teacher views of transfer student education. *American Educational Research Journal, 31*, 813–843. doi:10.3102/00028312031004813

Lashley, M., Maudry, B., Jeffers, A. E., & Davis, D. E. (2009). Psychosocial impact of mortgage foreclosure. *European Journal of Management, 9*(3). Retrieved from http://www.freepatentsonline.com/article/European-Journal-Management/260792631.html

Lavy, V., & Schlosser, A. (2011). Mechanisms and impacts of gender peer effects at school. *American Economic Journal: Applied Economics, American Economic Association, 3*(2), 1–33. Retrieved from http://www.nber.org/papers/w13292

Lazarus, R. S., & Folkman, S. (1984). *Stress, appraisal, and coping.* New York, NY: Springer.

Leedy, P. D., & Ormrod, J. E. (2010). *Practical research: Planning and design* (9th ed.). Upper Saddle River, NJ: Prentice-Hall.

Lovell, P., & Isaacs, J. (2008, April). The impact of the mortgage crisis on children and their education. Retrieved from http://www.brookings.edu/research/papers/2008 /05/04-mortgage-crisis-isaacs

Lubell, J., Crain, R., & Cohen, R. (2007, July). Framing the issues: The positive impact of affordable housing on health. Retrieved from http://www.nhc.org/pdf /chp_int_litrvw_hsghlth0707.pdf

Maddi, S. R., & Khoshaba, D. M. (2005, March). *Resilience at work: How to succeed no matter what life throws at you.* New York, NY: AMACOM.

Maikranz, J. M., Steele, R. G., & Forehand, R. (2003). Longitudinal correlates of depressive symptoms among urban African American children: II. Extension of findings across 3 years. *Journal of Clinical Child and Adolescent Psychology, 32*, 606–612. doi:10.1207/S15374424JCCP3204_14

Mallach, A. (2008, May 29). Tackling the mortgage crisis: 10 action steps for state government. Retrieved from http://www.brookings.edu/research/papers/2008/05 /29-mortgage- crisis-vey

Maslow, A. H. (1943). A theory of human motivation. *Psychological Review, 50*, 370–396. doi:10.1037/h0054346

Maxwell, L. E. (2003). Home and school density effects on elementary school children: The role of spatial density. *Environment and Behavior, 35*, 566–578. doi:10.1177/0013916503035004007

McEwen, K. (2011, July). *Building resilience at work*. Toowong, Queensland, Australia: Australian Academic Press.

Mehana, M., & Reynolds, A. J. (2004, January). School mobility and achievement: A meta-analysis. *Children and Youth Services Review, 26*, 93–119. doi:10.1016/j.childyouth.2003.11.004

Mental health: Keeping your emotional health. (2002, October 1). *American Family Physician, 66*, 1287–1288. Retrieved from http://www.aafp.org/afp/2002/1001/p1287.html

Miller, M. B., Leffingwell, T. R., Claborn, K., Meier, E., Walters, S., & Neighbors, C. (2012). Psychology of addictive behaviors : *Journal of the Society of Psychologists in Addictive Behaviors*, ISSN 0893-164X, 12/2013, Volume 27, Issue 4, p. 1101

Miroff, N. (2008, October 28). Foreclosures open door to disorder. *Washington Post*. Retrieved from http://www.washingtonpost.com

Moen, P. (1979). Family impact of the 1975 recession: Duration of unemployment. *Journal of Marriage and the Family, 41*, 561–572. Retrieved from http://www.jstor.org/discover/10.2307/351626?uid=3739672&uid=2129& uid=2&uid=70&uid=4&uid=3739256&sid=21102287872767

Moore, K., Vandivere, S., & Ehrle, J. (2000, June). Turbulence and child well-being. *New Federalism: National Survey of America's Families, Series B* (B-16). Retrieved from http://www.urban.org/UploadedPDF/anf_b16.pdf

Moos, R. H., Brennan, P. L., Schutte, K. K., & Moos, B. S. (2006). Older adults' coping with negative life events: Common processes of managing health, interpersonal, and financial/work stressors. *International Journal of Aging and Human Development, 62*, 39–59. doi:10.2190/ENLH-WAA2-AX8J-WRT1

Moreno, A. (1995, November). Cost effectiveness of mortgage foreclosure prevention: Summary of findings. Retrieved from http://www.fhfund.org/_dnld/reports/MFP_1995.pdf

Moustakas, C. E. (1994). *Phenomenological research methods*. Thousand Oaks, CA: Sage.

Mummolo, J., & Brubaker, B. (2008, April 27). As foreclosed homes empty, crime arrives. *Washington Post*. Retrieved from http://www.washingtonpost.com

National Alliance on Mental Illness. (2013). What is posttraumatic stress disorder (PTSD)? Retrieved from http://www.nami.org/ Template.cfm?Section=posttraumatic_stress_disorder

National Coalition for the Homeless. (2009, July). Why are people homeless? Retrieved from http://www.nationalhomeless.org/fact-sheets/Why.pdf

National Law Center on Homelessness and Poverty. (2010, June). Staying home: The rights of renters living in foreclosed properties. Retrieved from http://www.nlchp.org/content/pubs/ StayingHomeReport_June2010.pdf

National Low Income Housing Coalition. (2009). Without just cause: A 50-state review of the (lack of) rights of tenants in foreclosure. Retrieved from http://www.nlchp.org/content/pubs/Without_ Just_Cause1.pdf

Nebehay, S. (2008, October 9). Financial crisis may worsen mental health woes. Retrieved from http://www.reuters.com/article/2008/10/09/ us-financial-health-mental- idUSTRE49839M20081009

Nettleton, S., & Burrows, R. (2001, December). Families coping with the experience of mortgage repossession in the "new landscape of precariousness." *Community, Work and Family, 4*, 253–272. Retrieved from http://www.tandfonline.com/toc/ccwf20/cur-rent#.U5Ke5yimU1I

Ojeda, R., Jacquez, A., & Takash, C. (2009, October). The end of the American dream for Blacks and Latinos: How the home mortgage crisis is destroying Black and Latino wealth, jeopardizing America's future prosperity and how to fix it [White Paper]. Retrieved from http://www.wcvi.org/data/pub/housingwhitepaper061809.htm

Partnership for America's Economic Success. (2008, July). *Hidden costs of the housing crisis: The impact of housing on young children's odds of success* (Issue Brief No. 7). Retrieved from http://www.readyna-tion.org/docs/research_brief_200807 _housing.pdf

Pelletiere, D., & Wardrip, K. (2008). Renters and the housing credit crisis. *Poverty & Race, 17*(4). Retrieved from http://www.prrac. org/ full_text.php?text_id=1189&item_id=11271&newsletter_ id=100&header=Search% 20Results

Pence, K. M. (2006, February). Foreclosing on opportunity: State laws and mortgage credit. *Review of Economics and Statistics, 88*,

177–182. Retrieved from http://works.bepress.com/cgi/viewcontent.cgi?article=1001&context=karen_pene

Pettit, B. (2004). Moving and children's social connections: Neighborhood context and the consequences of moving for low income families. *Sociological Forum, 19*, 285–331. doi:10.1023/B:SOFO.0000031983.93817.ff

Pettit, K. L., Hendey, L., Kingsley, G. T., Cunningham, M., Comey, J., Getsinger, L., & Grosz, M. (2009). Housing in the nation's capital 2009. Retrieved from http://www.urban.org/UploadedPDF/1001340_housingnationscapital09.pdf

Phillips, D., Clark, R., Lee, T., & Desautels, A. (2010). Rebuilding neighborhoods restoring health: A report on the impact of foreclosures on public health. Retrieved from http://www.acphd.org/media/53643/foreclose2.pdf

Pollack, C. E., & Lynch, J. (2009). Health status of people undergoing foreclosure in the Philadelphia region. *American Journal of Public Health, 99*, 1833–1839. Retrieved from http://search.proquest.com/docview/215088649?accountid=35812

Public health; emerging public health crisis linked to mortgage default and foreclosure. (2011). *Investment Weekly News*, 364. Retrieved from http://search.proquest.com/docview/900514821?accountid=458

Rajendran, N. S. (2001). *Dealing with biases in qualitative research: A balancing act for researchers.* Paper presented at the Qualitative Research Convention 2001: Navigating Challenges, University of Malaya, Kuala Lumpur. Retrieved from http://nsrajendran.tripod.com/Papers/Qualconfe2001.pdf

Real Estate Webmasters Glossary. (n.d.). Foreclosure. Retrieved from http://www.realestatewebmasters.com/glossary/foreclosure/

Realty Trac (2013). National real estate trends & market info. Retrieved from http://www.realtytrac.com/statsandtrends/foreclosuretrends/NJ

Renzetti, C. M., & Edleson, J. L. (Eds.). (2008). *Encyclopedia of interpersonal violence* (Vols. 1–2). Thousand Oaks, CA: Sage. doi:10.4135/9781412963923

Riley, D., & Eckenrode, J. (1986). Social ties: Subgroup differences in costs and benefits. *Journal of Personality and Social Psychology, 51*, 772–778. doi:10.1037/0022-3514.51.4.770

Robertson, C., Egelhof, R., & Hoke, H. (2008, August 18). Get sick, get out: The medical causes of home mortgage foreclosures. *Health Matrix, 18*(65). Retrieved from http://law.cwru.edu/studentLife/organizations/healthmatrix/files/Robertson%	20Final%20 Article~1.pdf

Robinson, B., & Todd, R. M. (2010, June). *The role of non-owner-occupied homes in the current housing and foreclosure cycle* (Richmond Federal Bank Reserve Working Paper 10–11). Retrieved from http://www.richmondfed.org/publications/research	/working_ papers/2010/pdf/wp10-11.pdf

Rohe, W. M., & Stegman, M. A. (1994). The impact of home ownership on the social and political involvement of low-income people. *Urban Affairs Review, 30*, 152–172. doi:10.1177/004208169403000108

Rollins, G. (2003). Uncharitable care: Yale-New Haven hospital's charity care and collections practices. Retrieved from http://www.hospitaldebtjustice.org/unchar.pdf

Ross, C., & Huber, J. (1985, December). Hardship and depression. *Journal of Health and Social Behavior, 26*, 312–327. Retrieved from http://www.jstor.org/stable/2136655

Rowles, G. (1983). Between worlds: A relocation dilemma for the Appalachian elderly. *International Journal of Aging and Human Development, 17*, 301–314. doi:10.2190/X2UF-RQ0V-BLN5-GDCN

Rowles, G. D. (1993). Evolving images of place in aging and "Aging in Place": (Changing perceptions of aging and the aged). *Generations, 17*(2), 65–71. Retrieved from http://www.accessmylibrary.com/article/print/1G1-14035959

Saegert, S., Fields, D., & Libman, K. (2011). Mortgage foreclosure and health disparities: Serial displacement as asset extraction in african american populations. *Journal of Urban Health, 88*, 390–402. doi:10.1007/s11524-011-9584-3

Saunders, M., Lewis, P., & Thornhill, A. (2003). *Research methods for business students* (3rd ed.). Upper Saddle River, NJ: Prentice Hall.

Schneiderman, N., Ironson, G., & Siegel, S. D. (2005). Stress and health: Psychological, behavioral, and biological determinants. *Annual Review of Clinical Psychology 1*, 607–628. doi:10.1146/annurev.clinpsy.1.102803.144141

Schootman, M., Deshpande, A. D., Pruitt, S. L., & Jeffe, D. B. (2012). Neighborhood foreclosures and self-rated health among breast cancer survivors. *Quality of Life Research, 21*, 133–141. doi:10.1007/s11136-011-9929-0

Schroeder, M. (2006, March 30). Mortgage lenders dismiss concerns over risky loans. *Wall Street Journal.* Retrieved from http://online.wsj.com/

Schuetz, J., Been, V., & Ellen, I. G. (2008). Neighborhood effects of concentrated mortgage foreclosures. *Journal of Housing Economics, 17,* 306 319. doi:10.1016/j.jhe.2008.09.004

Scully, J., Tosi, H., & Banning, K. (2000). Life event checklists: Revisiting the social readjustment rating scale after 30 years. *Educational and Psychological Measurement 60,* 864. doi:10.1177/00131640021970952

Seifert, R. (2005, November). Home sick: How medical debt undermines housing security. Retrieved from http://www.accessproject.org/adobe/home_sick.pdf

Shelton, A. (2008, September 19). A first look at older Americans and the mortgage crisis. Retrieved from http://assets.aarp.org/rgcenter/econ/i9_mortgage.pdf

Shetty, A., & Kroleski, S. (2010, April). The mortgage crisis: Government intervention and debtors' options. *Journal of Business & Economics Research, 8*(4), 59–62 Retrieved from http://journals.cluteonline.com/index.php/JBER

Shortt, S. E. D. (1996). Is unemployment pathogenic? A review of current concepts with lessons for policy planners. *International Journal of Health Services, 26,* 569–589. doi:10.2190/DLYK-Q9W7-RRYX-8WKK

Singleton, T., George, L., Dickstein, C., & Thomas, H. (2006, Fall). *Subprime and predatory lending in rural America: Mortgage lending practices that can trap low income rural people* (Carsey Institute Policy Brief No. 4). Retrieved from http://www.carseyinstitute.unh.edu/publications/PB_predatorylending.pdf

Smith, R., & Ferryman, K. (2006). *Saying good-bye: Relocating senior citizens in the HOPE VI Panel Study* (Metropolitan Housing and Communities: A Roof Over Their Heads, Brief No. 10). Retrieved from http://www.urban.org/publications/311279.html

South, S. J., Haynie, D. L., & Bose, S. (2007). Student mobility and school dropout. *Social Science Research, 36,* 68–94. doi:10.1016/j.ssresearch.2005.10.001

Stein, C. H., & Makowski, E. S. (2004). Asking, witnessing, interpreting, knowing: Conducting qualitative research in community psychology. *American Journal of Community Psychology, 33,* 21. Retrieved from http://www.nbu.bg/webs/clubpsy/Materiali per t20za percent20kachvane/Library/razlichni percent20lekcii percent20na percent20angliiski/Community percent20Psychology percent20Research.pdf

Strauss, J., & Myburgh, C. P. H. (Eds.) (2001). *Research methodology study guide 81416.* Johannesburg, South Africa: Rand Afrikaans University.

Suicide; US foreclosures drive up suicide rate. (2014). *NewsRx Health & Science,*187. Retrieved from http://search.proquest.com/docview/1530107909?accountid=458

Tenants Together. (2009). Hidden impact: California renters in the foreclosure crisis. Retrieved from http://www.tenantstogether.org/downloads/ForeclosureReport.pdf

Treuhaft, S., Kalima, R., & Black, K. (2010, April). When investors buy up the neighborhood: Preventing investor ownership from causing neighborhood decline. Retrieved from http://www.policylink.org/atf/cf/%7B97c6d565-bb43-406d-a6d5-eca3bbf35af0%7D/WHENINVESTORSBUYUPTHENEIGHBORHOOD.PDF

Treves, G. (2010). Without justification: Banks continue mass displacement of innocent tenants after foreclosure. Retrieved from http://tenantstogether.org/downloads /Tenants% 20Together%20 Without%20Justifcation%20Report%20111810.pdf

Treves, G. (2011, January). California renters in the foreclosure crisis: Third annual report. Retrieved from http://www.tenantstogether.org/downloads/Third% 20Annual%20Report,%20 California%20Renters%20in%20the%20Foreclosure%20Crisis.pdf

U.S. Conference of Mayors. (2005). A status report on hunger and homelessness in America's cities. Retrieved from http://www.usmayors.org/hungersurvey/2005/HH2005FINAL.pdf

U.S. Department of Housing and Urban Development. (2013, July). Data sets: HUD provided local level data. Retrieved from http://www.huduser.org/portal/datasets/nsp_foreclosure_data.html

U.S. Department of Housing and Urban Development. (2013). Glossary. Retrieved from http://portal.hud.gov/hudportal/HUD?src=/program_offices/housing/sfh/buying/glossary

Wagner, A. W., Wolfe, J., Rotnitsky, A., Proctor, S. P., & Erickson, D. J. (2000). An investigation of the impact of posttraumatic stress disorder on physical health. *Journal of Traumatic Stress, 13*, 41–55. doi:10.1023/A:1007716813407

Waite, R. (2006). The psychiatric educational experiences of advance beginner RNs. *Nurse Education Today, 26*, 131–138. Retrieved from http://idea.library.drexel.edu/handle/1860/2624

Watson, S. D., Jorge, M., Cohen, A., & Seifert, R. W. (2007). Living in the red: Medical debt and housing security in Missouri. Retrieved from http://www.accessproject.org/adobe/living_in_the_red.pdf

Weich, S., & Lewis, G. (1998). Poverty, unemployment, and common mental disorders: Population based cohort study. *BMJ, 317*, 115–119. doi:10.1136/bmj.317.7151.115

Weinberg, B. (2007). *Social interactions and endogenous associations* (NBER Working Paper Series, Working Paper 13038). Retrieved from http://www.nber.org/papers/w13038.pdf

White, L. (2009, February 13). Renters, too, feeling effects of foreclosure crisis. *Contra Costa Times.* Retrieved from http://www.contracostatimes.com

Wisloski, J. (2008, February 17). Foreclosures in Jamaica now home to squatters, druggies—Making ghost town. *New York Daily News.* Retrieved from http://www.nydailynews.com

Woodard, J. (2012, July 30). Children: Primary victims of foreclosures. *Creators Syndicate.* Retrieved from http://search.proquest.com/docview/1030176833?accountid=458

Yin, R. K. (2009). *Case study research: Design and methods* (4th ed.). Los Angeles, CA: Sage. doi:10.1111/j.1540-4781.2011.01212_17.x

Zahavi, D. (2003). *Husserl's phenomenology.* Palo Alto, CA: Stanford University Press.

About the Author

Dr. Owusu Kizito

Dr. Owusu Kizito has a track record of being a dynamic, results-driven professional. He has close to twenty years of experience in consulting, banking, financial analysis, project management, and process improvement. In addition, he has an extensive background as analytic expert regarding the calculus of decision-making, and problem solving. Dr. Kizito has established an enviable track record of successfully designing solutions to difficult engagements and then coordinating their implementation. As a result he has been credited with creating, as well as maintaining lucrative client relationships. Dr. Owusu Kizito is the President and CEO of Investigroup Companies. He has successfully helped a lot of struggling homeowners retain their homes by applying his expert knowledge on foreclosure mitigation strategies with the banks and mortgage companies in a win-win scenario. Apart from being a housing counsel expert, he is also a tax expert helping taxpayers negotiate their tax obligations with the internal revenue service. Dr. Kizito holds an MBA from Hawaii Pacific University, postgraduate law certifications from Harvard University and a doctorate in Business Administration from the University of Phoenix. Dr. Kizito can be reached directly on (908) 977-7320 or email him at okizito@investigroup.org. Follow him on twitter for updates @okizito1.